KEITH BAXTER

A GOLFER'S NOTEBOOK

FRANCES LINCOLN LIMITED
PUBLISHERS

Frances Lincoln Limited
4 Torriano Mews
Torriano Avenue
London NW5 2RZ
www.franceslincoln.com

A Golfer's Notebook
Copyright © Frances Lincoln limited 2009
Text © Keith Baxter 2009
All photographs © Keith Baxter except where credited on page 152

All rights reserved. No part of this publication may be reproduced, stored in a
retrieval system or transmitted, in any form, or by any means, electronic,
mechanical, photocopying, recording or otherwise, without either prior
permission in writing from the publishers or a licence permitting restricted
copying. In the United Kingdom such licences are issued by the Copyright
Licensing Agency, Saffron House, 6–10 Kirby Street, London EC1N 8TS.

British Library cataloguing-in-publication data
A catalogue record for this book is available from the British Library

ISBN: 978-0-7112-2961-7

Printed in China
First Frances Lincoln edition 2009

Top 100 Checklists provided by Top 100 Golf Courses
(www.top100golfcourses.co.uk)
Every effort has been made to ensure that all the golf course information is
correct, however, neither the Publisher nor the Author can take any liability for
errors. Before making any special journeys always contact the golf course in
advance.

Front cover, endpapers and silhouettes: Courtesy of Shutterstock
This page: Turnberry (Ailsa), Scotland / © Anthony Munter

CONTENTS

INTRODUCTION

How many times have you paired up on the golf course with someone you didn't previously know, hit it off with them, scribbled their name and contact details on your scorecard at the end of the round and then promptly lost the card? How many times have you played a golf course and wished you'd taken a note of something special for future reference?

With a copy of *A Golfer's Notebook* in your golf bag, next to your sharpened pencil, you'll always have your personal golfing chronicle at hand and you'll never mislay that priceless snippet of information. I wish I'd owned *A Golfer's Notebook* years ago when I started my love affair with golf courses, as I've forgotten so much. Thankfully my memory is now improving!

The Top 100 checklists at the back of this notebook are probably aspirational for most people but they are inspirational for a few. I know a person who has played the Top 100 Golf Courses of the World. It took time, money and perseverance to achieve that feat but it was an incredible journey. I personally love playing world-class golf courses and I think it's a memorable experience for every golfer.

Use the checklists to tick off any Top 100 golf courses you've already played and use the lists as a focal point for future planning, but check the Top 100 website (www.top100golfcourses.co.uk) to find detailed information about these great top-ranked courses and hundreds of other lesser-known, unsung gems.

Keith Baxter
Editor
Top 100 Golf Courses

HOW TO USE THIS BOOK

A Golfer's Notebook is a flexible structured notebook designed by golfers *for* golfers.

Keeping your **Contacts** up-to-date will ensure you never lose details of people, professionals, favourite golf shops or websites.

The **Year Planners** enable planning for key events – whether it's a particular game, competition, trip or social or a major event on the golfing calendar. If you write in pencil you can make updates easily.

Competitions outlines some of the most popular competition formats that can be played individually or in pairs.

The **Handicap System** unravels the mystery of handicapping and also includes your own Handicap Calculator.

Measuring Your Yardage helps you work out how far you can hit the ball using different clubs. A bit of work getting to know your personal distances will reap dividends on the green.

Golfing Notes is a flexible space for you to use as you see fit – here you could make a note of your warm-up routines, jot down a tip from a golfing buddy or something you've read in a magazine. Whether or not you work with a pro, you might want to write up details of areas in your game to concentrate on in terms of short- and long-term goals. You might want to create a golfing wish list of equipment, magazines, books or dvds.

Round Score Records allow you to comment on specific games and record your scores.

Course Reviews are an opportunity to rate courses you visit so you'll know which ones you want to return to (as well as those you'd rather not).

Finally, the **Top 100 Checklists** for Britain and Ireland, North America and the World are tick lists of the very best golf courses you can aspire to play.

Kingsbarns (12th hole), Scotland

PERSONAL DETAILS

☺ ....

✉ ....

☎ ....
....

Golf Club Name: ....

✉ ....

☎ ....
....

Membership Secretary: ....

☎
💻 ....
....

Shop: ....

☎
💻 ....
....

Other Club Telephone Numbers:

....
....
....
....
....
....
....
....
....

CONTACTS

☺
☎
▤
💻

☺
☎
▤
💻

☺
☎
▤
💻

☺
☎
▤
💻

☺
☎
▤
💻

☺
☎
▤
💻

☺
☎
▤
💻

CONTACTS

☺
☎
▯
💻

☺
☎
▯
💻

☺
☎
▯
💻

☺
☎
▯
💻

☺
☎
▯
💻

☺
☎
▯
💻

☺
☎
▯
💻

☺
☎
🖩
💻

☺
☎
🖩
💻

☺
☎
🖩
💻

☺
☎
🖩
💻

☺
☎
🖩
💻

☺
☎
🖩
💻

☺
☎
🖩
💻

YEAR PLANNER

January	February
March	April
May	June
July	August
September	October
November	December

January	February
March	April
May	June
July	August
September	October
November	December

YEAR PLANNER

January	February
March	April
May	June
July	August
September	October
November	December

January	February
March	**April**
May	**June**
July	**August**
September	**October**
November	**December**

COMPETITIONS

One of golf's many delights is that there are several different types of competition, which – rather like tennis – may be played individually or in pairs. Outlined below are the four most popular competition formats:

Match Play – One of the original golf competitions is where a match consists of one side playing against another. The game is played on a hole-by-hole basis and the side that holes its ball in the fewer strokes wins the hole. Each hole is won, lost, or halved and the match is won when one side leads by a number of holes greater than the number remaining to be played.

Stroke Play – Consists of competitors completing each hole and returning a score for each hole. Each player is playing against every other player in the competition over a stipulated round or number of rounds. The player who completes the round or rounds in the fewest strokes is the winner.

Par or Bogey – A competition that scored similarly to Match Play where a hole is won, lost, or halved. But unlike Match Play, where the competition consists of one side playing against another, Par or Bogey consists of one side playing against the scorecard of the course. A hole is won by having a net score better than par, a hole is lost by having a net score worse than par and a hole is halved by having a net score equal to par. The player or team that wins the most holes against par is the winner.

Stableford – Dr Frank Stableford gave his name to the most popular points scoring competition system ever adopted. It's a competition with the objective of obtaining the highest points score. The Stableford system awards points relative to the net score against par of each hole:

0 points – more than one over par   3 points – one under par
1 point – one over par   2 points – par   4 points – two under par
                                      5 points – three under par

THE HANDICAP SYSTEM

The Council of National Golf Unions (CONGU®) was set up back in the 1920s by the Royal and Ancient Golf Club of St. Andrews (R&A) to define a uniform system of handicapping thereby allowing amateur players, male and female, of varying abilities to compete against each other on an equitable basis. In 2004 the ladies, who had used the LGU system until then, adopted the CONGU® UHS and now men and ladies are handicapped under the same system. Handicapping is a complicated business in its own right, but working out your correct handicap allowance for various competitions can also be a serious 1st tee challenge.

Handicap Allowances

CONGU® direct that the handicap allowances on the following page are used for the various forms of competition when played as handicap events and the reference to handicaps in all cases refers to Playing Handicaps.

For detailed information about handicaps, visit the CONGU® website at: www.congu.com
For information regarding competitions and the Rules of Golf visit the R&A website at: www.randa.org

Competition	Format	Handicap Allowances
Match Play	Singles	Full difference between the handicap of the players
Match Play	Foursomes	Half difference between aggregate handicaps of each side
Match Play	Four-ball	Lowest handicap player to concede strokes to the other 3 players based on three quarters of the difference between the full handicaps
Stroke Play	Singles	Full handicap
Stroke Play	Foursomes	Half aggregate handicap of partners
Stroke Play	Four-ball	Each partner receives three quarters of full handicap
Par or Bogey	Singles	Full handicap
Par or Bogey	Foursomes	Half aggregate handicap of partners
Par or Bogey	Four-ball	Each partner receives three quarters of full handicap
Stableford	Singles	Full handicap
Stableford	Foursomes	Half aggregate handicap of partners
Stableford	Four-ball	Each partner receives three quarters of full handicap

NB: Half strokes or over to be counted as one. Smaller fractions to be disregarded except in Foursomes Stroke Play when half strokes are counted as such.

Handicap Calculator

Difference	7/8	3/4	1/2	3/8	Difference	7/8	3/4	1/2	3/8
1	1	1	1	0	19	17	14	10	7
2	2	2	1	1	20	18	15	10	8
3	3	2	2	1	21	18	16	11	8
4	4	3	2	2	22	19	17	11	8
5	4	4	3	2	23	20	17	12	9
6	5	5	3	2	24	21	18	12	9
7	6	5	4	3	25	22	19	13	9
8	7	6	4	3	26	23	20	13	10
9	8	7	5	3	27	24	20	14	10
10	9	8	5	4	28	25	21	14	11
11	10	8	6	4	29	25	22	15	11
12	11	9	6	5	30	26	23	15	11
13	11	10	7	5	31	27	23	16	12
14	12	11	7	5	32	28	24	16	12
15	13	11	8	6	33	29	25	17	12
16	14	12	8	6	34	30	26	17	13
17	15	13	9	6	35	31	26	18	13
18	16	14	9	7	36	32	27	18	14

MEASURING YOUR YARDAGE

Few amateur golfers know how far they hit the ball with their own clubs and invariably leave approach shots short of the green. In order to pepper the pin you should spend a few hours down the range getting to know your personal distances.

The distance a golf ball travels with a given club depends on many things such as weather condition, your fitness, your swing speed, and how well your club head connects with the ball. To establish how far you hit the ball with each club in your bag, you should take your clubs to the practice ground (on a wind free day) and measure your yardage.

How to estimate your yardage for each of your clubs

Ideally, choose a wind free day
- Start off with the most elevated club in your bag, which will be either a lob wedge or sand wedge.
- Hit ten balls with your most lofted club.
- Ignore the two longest balls and the two shortest balls then average out the distance of the remaining six balls. The average figure becomes your personal yardage.
- Now continue this process, working your way upwards through every club in your bag through to your driver.

Record your yardage for each club on the chart (right). This will act as a good guide when you are out on the course removing your uncertainty around club selection. Repeat the exercise over time to see improvements.

The guideline range of yardages we've included approximate spans from a novices through to a professional, so the likelihood is that your personal yardage will fall somewhere in between.

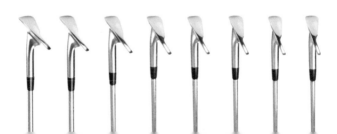

Club	Loft °	Novice	Professional	My Yardage		
Lob Wedge	60°	30 yd	90 yd			
Sand Wedge	56°	40 yd	110 yd			
Pitching Wedge	48°	60 yd	130 yd			
9 Iron	45°	80 yd	145 yd			
8 Iron	40°	90 yd	155 yd			
7 Iron	35°	100 yd	165 yd			
6 Iron	30°	110 yd	180 yd			
5 Iron	25°	120 yd	195 yd			
4 Iron	20°	130 yd	210 yd			
3 Iron	15°	140 yd	220 yd			
Hybrid	15–22°	145 yd	210+ yd			
5 Wood	14–16°	150 yd	210 yd			
3 Wood	13–15°	165 yd	230 yd			
Driver	8–11°	175 yd	250+ yd			

TAKING ACCOUNT OF THE WIND
Hitting into the wind (Headwind)
If you are hitting into a 10mph wind then you'll need to take at least one more club. Take at least two clubs more clubs for a 20mph headwind and so on.
Wind coming from behind (Tailwind)
If the 10mph wind is behind you take one less club. Take two less clubs for a 20mph tailwind and so on.

GOLFING NOTES

6/30/09

Lesson today w/ Brian, Assistant Pro at POXCC.

Ideas to remember:

(1) Practice swing before each shot

(2) Up hill lie. Set club face to target then play the shot; Weight on front foot

(3) Downhill lie. Same as above. Need to also swing along plane of downhill lie; Weight on front foot

(4) Swing thought - Pause at top of swing; release club and shoulder toward target; head focused on ball; shoulder will face head up after contact w/ ball

(5) Putting – Keep head down throughout swing; Also, take practice swing

(6) Fareway woods – set face square to ball; hands must be very loose – like holding a "bird"; finish swing forward – don't fall back

(7) All clubs – Don't fall back after you swing; must move forward; set body so weight ends up on left side.

(8) Play "bogey" golf
(bogey)

GOLFING NOTES

Ballybunion (Old), 18th hole, Ireland

GOLFING NOTES

GOLFING NOTES

....
....
....
....
....
....
....
....
....
....
....
....
....
....
....
....
....
....
....
....
....
....
....
....
....
....
....
....
....
....
....

Monte Mayor, Spain

GOLFING NOTES

Old Head (12th hole), Ireland

COURSE NAME ....

COMPETITION/EVENT ....

DATE .... TIME ....

GROSS SCORE .... HANDICAP .... NET SCORE .... STABLEFORD POINTS ....

Hole	1	2	3	4	5	6	7	8	9	Out	TOTAL
Yds/Mtrs											
Par											
Stroke Index											
My Score											
Hole	10	11	12	13	14	15	16	17	18	In	
Yds/Mtrs											
Par											
Stroke Index											
My Score											

COMMENTS (playing partners, weather, course condition, green fee, experiences etc.)

....
....
....
....
....
....
....
....
....
....
....
....

COURSE NAME ....

COMPETITION/EVENT ....

DATE .... TIME ....

GROSS SCORE .... HANDICAP .... NET SCORE .... STABLEFORD POINTS ....

Hole	1	2	3	4	5	6	7	8	9	Out	TOTAL
Yds/Mtrs											
Par											
Stroke Index											
My Score											
Hole	10	11	12	13	14	15	16	17	18	In	
Yds/Mtrs											
Par											
Stroke Index											
My Score											

COMMENTS (playing partners, weather, course condition, green fee, experiences etc.)

....
....
....
....
....
....
....
....
....
....
....
....

COURSE NAME ....

COMPETITION/EVENT ....

DATE .... TIME ....

GROSS SCORE .... HANDICAP .... NET SCORE .... STABLEFORD POINTS ....

Hole	1	2	3	4	5	6	7	8	9	Out	TOTAL
Yds/Mtrs											
Par											
Stroke Index											
My Score											
Hole	10	11	12	13	14	15	16	17	18	In	
Yds/Mtrs											
Par											
Stroke Index											
My Score											

COMMENTS (playing partners, weather, course condition, green fee, experiences etc.)

....
....
....
....
....
....
....
....
....
....
....
....
....

COURSE NAME ....

COMPETITION/EVENT ....

DATE .... TIME ....

GROSS SCORE .... HANDICAP .... NET SCORE .... STABLEFORD POINTS ....

Hole	1	2	3	4	5	6	7	8	9	Out	TOTAL
Yds/Mtrs											
Par											
Stroke Index											
My Score											
Hole	10	11	12	13	14	15	16	17	18	In	
Yds/Mtrs											
Par											
Stroke Index											
My Score											

COMMENTS (playing partners, weather, course condition, green fee, experiences etc.)

....
....
....
....
....
....
....
....
....
....
....
....
....

COURSE NAME ....

COMPETITION/EVENT ....

DATE .... TIME ....

GROSS SCORE .... HANDICAP .... NET SCORE .... STABLEFORD POINTS ....

Hole	1	2	3	4	5	6	7	8	9	Out	TOTAL
Yds/Mtrs											
Par											
Stroke Index											
My Score											
Hole	10	11	12	13	14	15	16	17	18	In	
Yds/Mtrs											
Par											
Stroke Index											
My Score											

COMMENTS (playing partners, weather, course condition, green fee, experiences etc.)

....
....
....
....
....
....
....
....
....
....
....
....

San Roque (Old), Spain

COURSE NAME ....

COMPETITION/EVENT ....

DATE .... TIME ....

GROSS SCORE .... HANDICAP .... NET SCORE .... STABLEFORD POINTS ....

Hole	1	2	3	4	5	6	7	8	9	Out	TOTAL
Yds/Mtrs											
Par											
Stroke Index											
My Score											
Hole	10	11	12	13	14	15	16	17	18	In	
Yds/Mtrs											
Par											
Stroke Index											
My Score											

COMMENTS (playing partners, weather, course condition, green fee, experiences etc.)

....
....
....
....
....
....
....
....
....
....
....
....

COURSE NAME ....

COMPETITION/EVENT ....

DATE .... TIME ....

GROSS SCORE .... HANDICAP .... NET SCORE .... STABLEFORD POINTS ....

Hole	1	2	3	4	5	6	7	8	9	Out	TOTAL
Yds/Mtrs											
Par											
Stroke Index											
My Score											
Hole	10	11	12	13	14	15	16	17	18	In	
Yds/Mtrs											
Par											
Stroke Index											
My Score											

COMMENTS (playing partners, weather, course condition, green fee, experiences etc.)

....
....
....
....
....
....
....
....
....
....
....
....
....

COURSE NAME ....

COMPETITION/EVENT ....

DATE .... TIME ....

GROSS SCORE .... HANDICAP .... NET SCORE .... STABLEFORD POINTS ....

Hole	1	2	3	4	5	6	7	8	9	Out	TOTAL
Yds/Mtrs											
Par											
Stroke Index											
My Score											
Hole	10	11	12	13	14	15	16	17	18	In	
Yds/Mtrs											
Par											
Stroke Index											
My Score											

COMMENTS (playing partners, weather, course condition, green fee, experiences etc.)

....
....
....
....
....
....
....
....
....
....
....

COURSE NAME ....

COMPETITION/EVENT ....

DATE .... TIME ....

GROSS SCORE .... HANDICAP .... NET SCORE .... STABLEFORD POINTS ....

Hole	1	2	3	4	5	6	7	8	9	Out	TOTAL
Yds/Mtrs											
Par											
Stroke Index											
My Score											
Hole	10	11	12	13	14	15	16	17	18	In	
Yds/Mtrs											
Par											
Stroke Index											
My Score											

COMMENTS (playing partners, weather, course condition, green fee, experiences etc.)

....
....
....
....
....
....
....
....
....
....
....
....
....

COURSE NAME ....

COMPETITION/EVENT ....

DATE .... TIME ....

GROSS SCORE .... HANDICAP .... NET SCORE .... STABLEFORD POINTS ....

Hole	1	2	3	4	5	6	7	8	9	Out	TOTAL
Yds/Mtrs											
Par											
Stroke Index											
My Score											
Hole	10	11	12	13	14	15	16	17	18	In	
Yds/Mtrs											
Par											
Stroke Index											
My Score											

COMMENTS (playing partners, weather, course condition, green fee, experiences etc.)

....
....
....
....
....
....
....
....
....
....
....
....

Prince's, England

COURSE NAME ....

COMPETITION/EVENT ....

DATE .... TIME ....

GROSS SCORE .... HANDICAP .... NET SCORE .... STABLEFORD POINTS ....

Hole	1	2	3	4	5	6	7	8	9	Out	TOTAL
Yds/Mtrs											
Par											
Stroke Index											
My Score											
Hole	10	11	12	13	14	15	16	17	18	In	
Yds/Mtrs											
Par											
Stroke Index											
My Score											

COMMENTS (playing partners, weather, course condition, green fee, experiences etc.)

....
....
....
....
....
....
....
....
....
....
....
....

COURSE NAME ....

COMPETITION/EVENT ....

DATE .... TIME ....

GROSS SCORE .... HANDICAP .... NET SCORE .... STABLEFORD POINTS ....

Hole	1	2	3	4	5	6	7	8	9	Out	TOTAL
Yds/Mtrs											
Par											
Stroke Index											
My Score											
Hole	10	11	12	13	14	15	16	17	18	In	
Yds/Mtrs											
Par											
Stroke Index											
My Score											

COMMENTS (playing partners, weather, course condition, green fee, experiences etc.)

....
....
....
....
....
....
....
....
....
....
....
....
....
....

COURSE NAME ....

COMPETITION/EVENT ....

DATE .... TIME ....

GROSS SCORE .... HANDICAP .... NET SCORE .... STABLEFORD POINTS ....

Hole	1	2	3	4	5	6	7	8	9	Out	TOTAL
Yds/Mtrs											
Par											
Stroke Index											
My Score											
Hole	10	11	12	13	14	15	16	17	18	In	
Yds/Mtrs											
Par											
Stroke Index											
My Score											

COMMENTS (playing partners, weather, course condition, green fee, experiences etc.)

....
....
....
....
....
....
....
....
....
....
....
....
....

COURSE NAME ....

COMPETITION/EVENT ....

DATE .... TIME ....

GROSS SCORE .... HANDICAP .... NET SCORE .... STABLEFORD POINTS ....

Hole	1	2	3	4	5	6	7	8	9	Out	TOTAL
Yds/Mtrs											
Par											
Stroke Index											
My Score											
Hole	10	11	12	13	14	15	16	17	18	In	
Yds/Mtrs											
Par											
Stroke Index											
My Score											

COMMENTS (playing partners, weather, course condition, green fee, experiences etc.)

....
....
....
....
....
....
....
....
....
....
....
....
....
....

COURSE NAME ....

COMPETITION/EVENT ....

DATE .... TIME ....

GROSS SCORE .... HANDICAP .... NET SCORE .... STABLEFORD POINTS ....

Hole	1	2	3	4	5	6	7	8	9	Out	TOTAL
Yds/Mtrs											
Par											
Stroke Index											
My Score											
Hole	10	11	12	13	14	15	16	17	18	In	
Yds/Mtrs											
Par											
Stroke Index											
My Score											

COMMENTS (playing partners, weather, course condition, green fee, experiences etc.)

....
....
....
....
....
....
....
....
....
....
....
....

COURSE NAME ....

COMPETITION/EVENT ....

DATE .... TIME ....

GROSS SCORE .... HANDICAP .... NET SCORE .... STABLEFORD POINTS ....

Hole	1	2	3	4	5	6	7	8	9	Out	TOTAL
Yds/Mtrs											
Par											
Stroke Index											
My Score											
Hole	10	11	12	13	14	15	16	17	18	In	
Yds/Mtrs											
Par											
Stroke Index											
My Score											

COMMENTS (playing partners, weather, course condition, green fee, experiences etc.)

....
....
....
....
....
....
....
....
....
....
....
....

COURSE NAME ....

COMPETITION/EVENT ....

DATE .... TIME ....

GROSS SCORE .... HANDICAP .... NET SCORE .... STABLEFORD POINTS ....

Hole	1	2	3	4	5	6	7	8	9	Out	TOTAL
Yds/Mtrs											
Par											
Stroke Index											
My Score											
Hole	10	11	12	13	14	15	16	17	18	In	
Yds/Mtrs											
Par											
Stroke Index											
My Score											

COMMENTS (playing partners, weather, course condition, green fee, experiences etc.)

....
....
....
....
....
....
....
....
....
....
....
....
....

Dooks (15th hole), Ireland

COURSE NAME ....

COMPETITION/EVENT ....

DATE .... TIME ....

GROSS SCORE .... HANDICAP .... NET SCORE .... STABLEFORD POINTS ....

Hole	1	2	3	4	5	6	7	8	9	Out	TOTAL
Yds/Mtrs											
Par											
Stroke Index											
My Score											
Hole	10	11	12	13	14	15	16	17	18	In	
Yds/Mtrs											
Par											
Stroke Index											
My Score											

COMMENTS (playing partners, weather, course condition, green fee, experiences etc.)

....
....
....
....
....
....
....
....
....
....
....
....
....

COURSE NAME ....

COMPETITION/EVENT ....

DATE .... TIME ....

GROSS SCORE .... HANDICAP .... NET SCORE .... STABLEFORD POINTS ....

Hole	1	2	3	4	5	6	7	8	9	Out	TOTAL
Yds/Mtrs											
Par											
Stroke Index											
My Score											
Hole	10	11	12	13	14	15	16	17	18	In	
Yds/Mtrs											
Par											
Stroke Index											
My Score											

COMMENTS (playing partners, weather, course condition, green fee, experiences etc.)

....
....
....
....
....
....
....
....
....
....
....
....

COURSE NAME ....

COMPETITION/EVENT ....

DATE .... TIME ....

GROSS SCORE .... HANDICAP .... NET SCORE .... STABLEFORD POINTS ....

Hole	1	2	3	4	5	6	7	8	9	Out	TOTAL
Yds/Mtrs											
Par											
Stroke Index											
My Score											
Hole	10	11	12	13	14	15	16	17	18	In	
Yds/Mtrs											
Par											
Stroke Index											
My Score											

COMMENTS (playing partners, weather, course condition, green fee, experiences etc.)

....
....
....
....
....
....
....
....
....
....
....
....

COURSE NAME ....

COMPETITION/EVENT ....

DATE .... TIME ....

GROSS SCORE .... HANDICAP .... NET SCORE .... STABLEFORD POINTS ....

Hole	1	2	3	4	5	6	7	8	9	Out	TOTAL
Yds/Mtrs											
Par											
Stroke Index											
My Score											
Hole	10	11	12	13	14	15	16	17	18	In	
Yds/Mtrs											
Par											
Stroke Index											
My Score											

COMMENTS (playing partners, weather, course condition, green fee, experiences etc.)

....
....
....
....
....
....
....
....
....
....
....
....

COURSE NAME ....

COMPETITION/EVENT ....

DATE .... TIME ....

GROSS SCORE .... HANDICAP .... NET SCORE .... STABLEFORD POINTS ....

Hole	1	2	3	4	5	6	7	8	9	Out	TOTAL
Yds/Mtrs											
Par											
Stroke Index											
My Score											
Hole	10	11	12	13	14	15	16	17	18	In	
Yds/Mtrs											
Par											
Stroke Index											
My Score											

COMMENTS (playing partners, weather, course condition, green fee, experiences etc.)

....
....
....
....
....
....
....
....
....
....
....
....

Gloria Resort, Turkey

COURSE NAME ....

COMPETITION/EVENT ....

DATE .... TIME ....

GROSS SCORE .... HANDICAP .... NET SCORE .... STABLEFORD POINTS ....

Hole	1	2	3	4	5	6	7	8	9	Out	TOTAL
Yds/Mtrs											
Par											
Stroke Index											
My Score											
Hole	10	11	12	13	14	15	16	17	18	In	
Yds/Mtrs											
Par											
Stroke Index											
My Score											

COMMENTS (playing partners, weather, course condition, green fee, experiences etc.)

....
....
....
....
....
....
....
....
....
....
....

COURSE NAME ....

COMPETITION/EVENT ....

DATE .... TIME ....

GROSS SCORE .... HANDICAP .... NET SCORE .... STABLEFORD POINTS ....

Hole	1	2	3	4	5	6	7	8	9	Out	TOTAL
Yds/Mtrs											
Par											
Stroke Index											
My Score											
Hole	10	11	12	13	14	15	16	17	18	In	
Yds/Mtrs											
Par											
Stroke Index											
My Score											

COMMENTS (playing partners, weather, course condition, green fee, experiences etc.)

....
....
....
....
....
....
....
....
....
....
....
....

COURSE NAME ....

COMPETITION/EVENT ....

DATE .... TIME ....

GROSS SCORE .... HANDICAP .... NET SCORE .... STABLEFORD POINTS ....

Hole	1	2	3	4	5	6	7	8	9	Out	TOTAL
Yds/Mtrs											
Par											
Stroke Index											
My Score											
Hole	10	11	12	13	14	15	16	17	18	In	
Yds/Mtrs											
Par											
Stroke Index											
My Score											

COMMENTS (playing partners, weather, course condition, green fee, experiences etc.)

....
....
....
....
....
....
....
....
....
....
....
....

COURSE NAME ....

COMPETITION/EVENT ....

DATE .... TIME ....

GROSS SCORE .... HANDICAP .... NET SCORE .... STABLEFORD POINTS ....

Hole	1	2	3	4	5	6	7	8	9	Out	TOTAL
Yds/Mtrs											
Par											
Stroke Index											
My Score											
Hole	10	11	12	13	14	15	16	17	18	In	
Yds/Mtrs											
Par											
Stroke Index											
My Score											

COMMENTS (playing partners, weather, course condition, green fee, experiences etc.)

....
....
....
....
....
....
....
....
....
....
....
....

COURSE NAME ....

COMPETITION/EVENT ....

DATE .... TIME ....

GROSS SCORE .... HANDICAP .... NET SCORE .... STABLEFORD POINTS ....

Hole	1	2	3	4	5	6	7	8	9	Out	TOTAL
Yds/Mtrs											
Par											
Stroke Index											
My Score											
Hole	10	11	12	13	14	15	16	17	18	In	
Yds/Mtrs											
Par											
Stroke Index											
My Score											

COMMENTS (playing partners, weather, course condition, green fee, experiences etc.)

....
....
....
....
....
....
....
....
....
....
....
....

Finca Cortesin, Spain

COURSE NAME ....

COMPETITION/EVENT ....

DATE .... TIME ....

GROSS SCORE .... HANDICAP .... NET SCORE .... STABLEFORD POINTS ....

Hole	1	2	3	4	5	6	7	8	9	Out	TOTAL
Yds/Mtrs											
Par											
Stroke Index											
My Score											
Hole	10	11	12	13	14	15	16	17	18	In	
Yds/Mtrs											
Par											
Stroke Index											
My Score											

COMMENTS (playing partners, weather, course condition, green fee, experiences etc.)

....
....
....
....
....
....
....
....
....
....
....
....

COURSE NAME ....

COMPETITION/EVENT ....

DATE .... TIME ....

GROSS SCORE .... HANDICAP .... NET SCORE .... STABLEFORD POINTS ....

Hole	1	2	3	4	5	6	7	8	9	Out	TOTAL
Yds/Mtrs											
Par											
Stroke Index											
My Score											
Hole	10	11	12	13	14	15	16	17	18	In	
Yds/Mtrs											
Par											
Stroke Index											
My Score											

COMMENTS (playing partners, weather, course condition, green fee, experiences etc.)

....

....

....

....

....

....

....

....

....

....

....

....

COURSE NAME ....

COMPETITION/EVENT ....

DATE .... TIME ....

GROSS SCORE .... HANDICAP .... NET SCORE .... STABLEFORD POINTS ....

Hole	1	2	3	4	5	6	7	8	9	Out	TOTAL
Yds/Mtrs											
Par											
Stroke Index											
My Score											
Hole	10	11	12	13	14	15	16	17	18	In	
Yds/Mtrs											
Par											
Stroke Index											
My Score											

COMMENTS (playing partners, weather, course condition, green fee, experiences etc.)

....
....
....
....
....
....
....
....
....
....
....

COURSE NAME ....

COMPETITION/EVENT ....

DATE .... TIME ....

GROSS SCORE .... HANDICAP .... NET SCORE .... STABLEFORD POINTS ....

Hole	1	2	3	4	5	6	7	8	9	Out	TOTAL
Yds/Mtrs											
Par											
Stroke Index											
My Score											
Hole	10	11	12	13	14	15	16	17	18	In	
Yds/Mtrs											
Par											
Stroke Index											
My Score											

COMMENTS (playing partners, weather, course condition, green fee, experiences etc.)

....
....
....
....
....
....
....
....
....
....
....
....
....

COURSE NAME ....

COMPETITION/EVENT ....

DATE .... TIME ....

GROSS SCORE .... HANDICAP .... NET SCORE .... STABLEFORD POINTS ....

Hole	1	2	3	4	5	6	7	8	9	Out	TOTAL
Yds/Mtrs											
Par											
Stroke Index											
My Score											
Hole	10	11	12	13	14	15	16	17	18	In	
Yds/Mtrs											
Par											
Stroke Index											
My Score											

COMMENTS (playing partners, weather, course condition, green fee, experiences etc.)

....
....
....
....
....
....
....
....
....
....
....
....

COURSE NAME ....

COMPETITION/EVENT ....

DATE .... TIME ....

GROSS SCORE .... HANDICAP .... NET SCORE .... STABLEFORD POINTS ....

Hole	1	2	3	4	5	6	7	8	9	Out	TOTAL
Yds/Mtrs											
Par											
Stroke Index											
My Score											
Hole	10	11	12	13	14	15	16	17	18	In	
Yds/Mtrs											
Par											
Stroke Index											
My Score											

COMMENTS (playing partners, weather, course condition, green fee, experiences etc.)

....
....
....
....
....
....
....
....
....
....
....
....
....

COURSE NAME ....

COMPETITION/EVENT ....

DATE .... TIME ....

GROSS SCORE .... HANDICAP .... NET SCORE .... STABLEFORD POINTS ....

Hole	1	2	3	4	5	6	7	8	9	Out	TOTAL
Yds/Mtrs											
Par											
Stroke Index											
My Score											
Hole	10	11	12	13	14	15	16	17	18	In	
Yds/Mtrs											
Par											
Stroke Index											
My Score											

COMMENTS (playing partners, weather, course condition, green fee, experiences etc.)

....
....
....
....
....
....
....
....
....
....
....
....
....

Abama, Tenerife

COURSE NAME ....

COMPETITION/EVENT ....

DATE .... TIME ....

GROSS SCORE .... HANDICAP .... NET SCORE .... STABLEFORD POINTS ....

Hole	1	2	3	4	5	6	7	8	9	Out	TOTAL
Yds/Mtrs											
Par											
Stroke Index											
My Score											
Hole	10	11	12	13	14	15	16	17	18	In	
Yds/Mtrs											
Par											
Stroke Index											
My Score											

COMMENTS (playing partners, weather, course condition, green fee, experiences etc.)

....
....
....
....
....
....
....
....
....
....
....
....
....

COURSE NAME ....

COMPETITION/EVENT ....

DATE .... TIME ....

GROSS SCORE .... HANDICAP .... NET SCORE .... STABLEFORD POINTS ....

Hole	1	2	3	4	5	6	7	8	9	Out	TOTAL
Yds/Mtrs											
Par											
Stroke Index											
My Score											
Hole	10	11	12	13	14	15	16	17	18	In	
Yds/Mtrs											
Par											
Stroke Index											
My Score											

COMMENTS (playing partners, weather, course condition, green fee, experiences etc.)

....
....
....
....
....
....
....
....
....
....
....
....

COURSE NAME ....

COMPETITION/EVENT ....

DATE .... TIME ....

GROSS SCORE .... HANDICAP .... NET SCORE .... STABLEFORD POINTS ....

Hole	1	2	3	4	5	6	7	8	9	Out	TOTAL
Yds/Mtrs											
Par											
Stroke Index											
My Score											
Hole	10	11	12	13	14	15	16	17	18	In	
Yds/Mtrs											
Par											
Stroke Index											
My Score											

COMMENTS (playing partners, weather, course condition, green fee, experiences etc.)

....
....
....
....
....
....
....
....
....
....
....
....

COURSE NAME ....

COMPETITION/EVENT ....

DATE .... TIME ....

GROSS SCORE .... HANDICAP .... NET SCORE .... STABLEFORD POINTS ....

Hole	1	2	3	4	5	6	7	8	9	Out	TOTAL
Yds/Mtrs											
Par											
Stroke Index											
My Score											
Hole	10	11	12	13	14	15	16	17	18	In	
Yds/Mtrs											
Par											
Stroke Index											
My Score											

COMMENTS (playing partners, weather, course condition, green fee, experiences etc.)

....
....
....
....
....
....
....
....
....
....
....
....

COURSE NAME ....

COMPETITION/EVENT ....

DATE .... TIME ....

GROSS SCORE .... HANDICAP .... NET SCORE .... STABLEFORD POINTS ....

Hole	1	2	3	4	5	6	7	8	9	Out	TOTAL
Yds/Mtrs											
Par											
Stroke Index											
My Score											
Hole	10	11	12	13	14	15	16	17	18	In	
Yds/Mtrs											
Par											
Stroke Index											
My Score											

COMMENTS (playing partners, weather, course condition, green fee, experiences etc.)

....
....
....
....
....
....
....
....
....
....
....
....
....

Walton Heath (Old), England

COURSE NAME ....

COMPETITION/EVENT ....

DATE .... TIME ....

GROSS SCORE .... HANDICAP .... NET SCORE .... STABLEFORD POINTS ....

Hole	1	2	3	4	5	6	7	8	9	Out	TOTAL
Yds/Mtrs											
Par											
Stroke Index											
My Score											
Hole	10	11	12	13	14	15	16	17	18	In	
Yds/Mtrs											
Par											
Stroke Index											
My Score											

COMMENTS (playing partners, weather, course condition, green fee, experiences etc.)

....
....
....
....
....
....
....
....
....
....
....
....
....

COURSE NAME ....

COMPETITION/EVENT ....

DATE .... TIME ....

GROSS SCORE .... HANDICAP .... NET SCORE .... STABLEFORD POINTS ....

Hole	1	2	3	4	5	6	7	8	9	Out	TOTAL
Yds/Mtrs											
Par											
Stroke Index											
My Score											
Hole	10	11	12	13	14	15	16	17	18	In	
Yds/Mtrs											
Par											
Stroke Index											
My Score											

COMMENTS (playing partners, weather, course condition, green fee, experiences etc.)

....
....
....
....
....
....
....
....
....
....
....
....
....

COURSE NAME ....

COMPETITION/EVENT ....

DATE .... TIME ....

GROSS SCORE .... HANDICAP .... NET SCORE .... STABLEFORD POINTS ....

Hole	1	2	3	4	5	6	7	8	9	Out	TOTAL
Yds/Mtrs											
Par											
Stroke Index											
My Score											
Hole	10	11	12	13	14	15	16	17	18	In	
Yds/Mtrs											
Par											
Stroke Index											
My Score											

COMMENTS (playing partners, weather, course condition, green fee, experiences etc.)

....
....
....
....
....
....
....
....
....
....
....
....

COURSE NAME ....

COMPETITION/EVENT ....

DATE .... TIME ....

GROSS SCORE .... HANDICAP .... NET SCORE .... STABLEFORD POINTS ....

Hole	1	2	3	4	5	6	7	8	9	Out	TOTAL
Yds/Mtrs											
Par											
Stroke Index											
My Score											
Hole	10	11	12	13	14	15	16	17	18	In	
Yds/Mtrs											
Par											
Stroke Index											
My Score											

COMMENTS (playing partners, weather, course condition, green fee, experiences etc.)

....
....
....
....
....
....
....
....
....
....
....
....
....

COURSE NAME ....

COMPETITION/EVENT ....

DATE .... TIME ....

GROSS SCORE .... HANDICAP .... NET SCORE .... STABLEFORD POINTS ....

Hole	1	2	3	4	5	6	7	8	9	Out	TOTAL
Yds/Mtrs											
Par											
Stroke Index											
My Score											
Hole	10	11	12	13	14	15	16	17	18	In	
Yds/Mtrs											
Par											
Stroke Index											
My Score											

COMMENTS (playing partners, weather, course condition, green fee, experiences etc.)

....
....
....
....
....
....
....
....
....
....
....
....

Lahinch (Old), Ireland

COURSE NAME ....

COMPETITION/EVENT ....

DATE .... TIME ....

GROSS SCORE .... HANDICAP .... NET SCORE .... STABLEFORD POINTS ....

Hole	1	2	3	4	5	6	7	8	9	Out	TOTAL
Yds/Mtrs											
Par											
Stroke Index											
My Score											
Hole	10	11	12	13	14	15	16	17	18	In	
Yds/Mtrs											
Par											
Stroke Index											
My Score											

COMMENTS (playing partners, weather, course condition, green fee, experiences etc.)

....
....
....
....
....
....
....
....
....
....
....
....

COURSE NAME ....

COMPETITION/EVENT ....

DATE .... TIME ....

GROSS SCORE .... HANDICAP .... NET SCORE .... STABLEFORD POINTS ....

Hole	1	2	3	4	5	6	7	8	9	Out	TOTAL
Yds/Mtrs											
Par											
Stroke Index											
My Score											
Hole	10	11	12	13	14	15	16	17	18	In	
Yds/Mtrs											
Par											
Stroke Index											
My Score											

COMMENTS (playing partners, weather, course condition, green fee, experiences etc.)

....
....
....
....
....
....
....
....
....
....
....
....

COURSE NAME ....

COMPETITION/EVENT ....

DATE .... TIME ....

GROSS SCORE .... HANDICAP .... NET SCORE .... STABLEFORD POINTS ....

Hole	1	2	3	4	5	6	7	8	9	Out	TOTAL
Yds/Mtrs											
Par											
Stroke Index											
My Score											
Hole	10	11	12	13	14	15	16	17	18	In	
Yds/Mtrs											
Par											
Stroke Index											
My Score											

COMMENTS (playing partners, weather, course condition, green fee, experiences etc.)

....
....
....
....
....
....
....
....
....
....
....
....

COURSE NAME ....

COMPETITION/EVENT ....

DATE .... TIME ....

GROSS SCORE .... HANDICAP .... NET SCORE .... STABLEFORD POINTS ....

Hole	1	2	3	4	5	6	7	8	9	Out	TOTAL
Yds/Mtrs											
Par											
Stroke Index											
My Score											
Hole	10	11	12	13	14	15	16	17	18	In	
Yds/Mtrs											
Par											
Stroke Index											
My Score											

COMMENTS (playing partners, weather, course condition, green fee, experiences etc.)

....

....

....

....

....

....

....

....

....

....

....

....

COURSE NAME ....

COMPETITION/EVENT ....

DATE .... TIME ....

GROSS SCORE .... HANDICAP .... NET SCORE .... STABLEFORD POINTS ....

Hole	1	2	3	4	5	6	7	8	9	Out	TOTAL
Yds/Mtrs											
Par											
Stroke Index											
My Score											
Hole	10	11	12	13	14	15	16	17	18	In	
Yds/Mtrs											
Par											
Stroke Index											
My Score											

COMMENTS (playing partners, weather, course condition, green fee, experiences etc.)

....
....
....
....
....
....
....
....
....
....
....
....
....

Santana (1st hole), Spain

COURSE NAME ....

COMPETITION/EVENT ....

DATE .... TIME ....

GROSS SCORE .... HANDICAP .... NET SCORE .... STABLEFORD POINTS ....

Hole	1	2	3	4	5	6	7	8	9	Out	TOTAL
Yds/Mtrs											
Par											
Stroke Index											
My Score											
Hole	10	11	12	13	14	15	16	17	18	In	
Yds/Mtrs											
Par											
Stroke Index											
My Score											

COMMENTS (playing partners, weather, course condition, green fee, experiences etc.)

....
....
....
....
....
....
....
....
....
....
....
....

COURSE NAME ....

COMPETITION/EVENT ....

DATE .... TIME ....

GROSS SCORE .... HANDICAP .... NET SCORE .... STABLEFORD POINTS ....

Hole	1	2	3	4	5	6	7	8	9	Out	TOTAL
Yds/Mtrs											
Par											
Stroke Index											
My Score											
Hole	10	11	12	13	14	15	16	17	18	In	
Yds/Mtrs											
Par											
Stroke Index											
My Score											

COMMENTS (playing partners, weather, course condition, green fee, experiences etc.)

....
....
....
....
....
....
....
....
....
....
....
....
....

COURSE NAME ....

COMPETITION/EVENT ....

DATE .... TIME ....

GROSS SCORE .... HANDICAP .... NET SCORE .... STABLEFORD POINTS ....

Hole	1	2	3	4	5	6	7	8	9	Out	TOTAL
Yds/Mtrs											
Par											
Stroke Index											
My Score											
Hole	10	11	12	13	14	15	16	17	18	In	
Yds/Mtrs											
Par											
Stroke Index											
My Score											

COMMENTS (playing partners, weather, course condition, green fee, experiences etc.)

....

....

....

....

....

....

....

....

....

....

....

COURSE NAME ....

COMPETITION/EVENT ....

DATE .... TIME ....

GROSS SCORE .... HANDICAP .... NET SCORE .... STABLEFORD POINTS ....

Hole	1	2	3	4	5	6	7	8	9	Out	TOTAL
Yds/Mtrs											
Par											
Stroke Index											
My Score											
Hole	10	11	12	13	14	15	16	17	18	In	
Yds/Mtrs											
Par											
Stroke Index											
My Score											

COMMENTS (playing partners, weather, course condition, green fee, experiences etc.)

....
....
....
....
....
....
....
....
....
....
....
....

COURSE NAME ....

COMPETITION/EVENT ....

DATE .... TIME ....

GROSS SCORE .... HANDICAP .... NET SCORE .... STABLEFORD POINTS ....

Hole	1	2	3	4	5	6	7	8	9	Out	TOTAL
Yds/Mtrs											
Par											
Stroke Index											
My Score											
Hole	10	11	12	13	14	15	16	17	18	In	
Yds/Mtrs											
Par											
Stroke Index											
My Score											

COMMENTS (playing partners, weather, course condition, green fee, experiences etc.)

....
....
....
....
....
....
....
....
....
....
....
....

Moor Park clubhouse, England

COURSE NAME ....

COMPETITION/EVENT ....

DATE .... TIME ....

GROSS SCORE .... HANDICAP .... NET SCORE .... STABLEFORD POINTS ....

Hole	1	2	3	4	5	6	7	8	9	Out	TOTAL
Yds/Mtrs											
Par											
Stroke Index											
My Score											
Hole	10	11	12	13	14	15	16	17	18	In	
Yds/Mtrs											
Par											
Stroke Index											
My Score											

COMMENTS (playing partners, weather, course condition, green fee, experiences etc.)

....
....
....
....
....
....
....
....
....
....
....
....

COURSE NAME ....

COMPETITION/EVENT ....

DATE .... TIME ....

GROSS SCORE .... HANDICAP .... NET SCORE .... STABLEFORD POINTS ....

Hole	1	2	3	4	5	6	7	8	9	Out	TOTAL
Yds/Mtrs											
Par											
Stroke Index											
My Score											
Hole	10	11	12	13	14	15	16	17	18	In	
Yds/Mtrs											
Par											
Stroke Index											
My Score											

COMMENTS (playing partners, weather, course condition, green fee, experiences etc.)

....
....
....
....
....
....
....
....
....
....
....
....

COURSE NAME ....

COMPETITION/EVENT ....

DATE .... TIME ....

GROSS SCORE .... HANDICAP .... NET SCORE .... STABLEFORD POINTS ....

Hole	1	2	3	4	5	6	7	8	9	Out	TOTAL
Yds/Mtrs											
Par											
Stroke Index											
My Score											
Hole	10	11	12	13	14	15	16	17	18	In	
Yds/Mtrs											
Par											
Stroke Index											
My Score											

COMMENTS (playing partners, weather, course condition, green fee, experiences etc.)

....
....
....
....
....
....
....
....
....
....
....
....

COURSE NAME ....

COMPETITION/EVENT ....

DATE .... TIME ....

GROSS SCORE .... HANDICAP .... NET SCORE ....STABLEFORD POINTS ....

Hole	1	2	3	4	5	6	7	8	9	Out	TOTAL
Yds/Mtrs											
Par											
Stroke Index											
My Score											
Hole	10	11	12	13	14	15	16	17	18	In	
Yds/Mtrs											
Par											
Stroke Index											
My Score											

COMMENTS (playing partners, weather, course condition, green fee, experiences etc.)

....
....
....
....
....
....
....
....
....
....
....
....

Brocket Hall Melbourne (18th hole), England

COURSE REVIEW

Course name: **Address:** **Website:** **Telephone:** **Contacts:** **Email:**	**OVERALL RATING:** ✪ ✪ ✪ ✪ ✪ **Course rating:** ✪ ✪ ✪ ✪ ✪ **Shop rating:** ✪ ✪ ✪ ✪ ✪ **Bar/Restaurant rating:** ✪ ✪ ✪ ✪ ✪ **Staff rating:** ✪ ✪ ✪ ✪ ✪
Shop: yes○ no○ Telephone: **Lessons:** yes○ no○ Telephone: **Carts for hire:** yes○ no○ **Practice range:** yes○ no○ **Practice greens:** yes○ no○	**Par:** **No. of holes:** **Av. time complete round:** **Green fees:**
	Restaurant/bar: yes○ no○ Telephone: *Comments*:
Comments:	

COURSE REVIEW

Course name: **Address:** **Website:** **Telephone:** **Contacts:** **Email:**	**OVERALL RATING:** ✪ ✪ ✪ ✪ ✪ **Course rating:** ✪ ✪ ✪ ✪ ✪ **Shop rating:** ✪ ✪ ✪ ✪ ✪ **Bar/Restaurant rating:** ✪ ✪ ✪ ✪ ✪ **Staff rating:** ✪ ✪ ✪ ✪ ✪
Shop: yes○ no○ Telephone: **Lessons:** yes○ no○ Telephone: **Carts for hire:** yes○ no○ **Practice range:** yes○ no○ **Practice greens:** yes○ no○	**Par:** **No. of holes:** **Av. time complete round:** **Green fees:**
	Restaurant/bar: yes○ no○ Telephone: *Comments*:
Comments:	

105

COURSE REVIEW

Course name: **Address:** **Website:** **Telephone:** **Contacts:** **Email:**	**OVERALL RATING:** ✪ ✪ ✪ ✪ ✪ **Course rating:** ✪ ✪ ✪ ✪ ✪ **Shop rating:** ✪ ✪ ✪ ✪ ✪ **Bar/Restaurant rating:** ✪ ✪ ✪ ✪ ✪ **Staff rating:** ✪ ✪ ✪ ✪ ✪

Shop: yes◯ no◯
Telephone:
Lessons: yes◯ no◯
Telephone:
Carts for hire: yes◯ no◯
Practice range: yes◯ no◯
Practice greens: yes◯ no◯

Par:
No. of holes:
Av. time complete round:
Green fees:

Restaurant/bar: yes◯ no◯
Telephone:
Comments:

Comments:

COURSE REVIEW

Course name: **Address:** **Website:** **Telephone:** **Contacts:** **Email:**	**OVERALL RATING:** ✪ ✪ ✪ ✪ ✪ **Course rating:** ✪ ✪ ✪ ✪ ✪ **Shop rating:** ✪ ✪ ✪ ✪ ✪ **Bar/Restaurant rating:** ✪ ✪ ✪ ✪ ✪ **Staff rating:** ✪ ✪ ✪ ✪ ✪
Shop: yes ◯ no ◯ Telephone: **Lessons:** yes ◯ no ◯ Telephone: **Carts for hire:** yes ◯ no ◯ **Practice range:** yes ◯ no ◯ **Practice greens:** yes ◯ no ◯	**Par:** **No. of holes:** **Av. time complete round:** **Green fees:**
	Restaurant/bar: yes ◯ no ◯ Telephone: *Comments*:

Comments:

COURSE REVIEW

Course name: **Address:** **Website:** **Telephone:** **Contacts:** **Email:**	**OVERALL RATING:** ✪ ✪ ✪ ✪ ✪ **Course rating:** ✪ ✪ ✪ ✪ ✪ **Shop rating:** ✪ ✪ ✪ ✪ ✪ **Bar/Restaurant rating:** ✪ ✪ ✪ ✪ ✪ **Staff rating:** ✪ ✪ ✪ ✪ ✪

Shop: yes○ no○ Telephone: **Lessons:** yes○ no○ Telephone: **Carts for hire:** yes○ no○ **Practice range:** yes○ no○ **Practice greens:** yes○ no○	**Par:** **No. of holes:** **Av. time complete round:** **Green fees:**
	Restaurant/bar: yes○ no○ Telephone: *Comments*:

Comments:

St. Enodoc (Church), England

COURSE REVIEW

Course name:	**OVERALL RATING:** ✪ ✪ ✪ ✪ ✪
Address:	
	Course rating: ✪ ✪ ✪ ✪ ✪
	Shop rating: ✪ ✪ ✪ ✪ ✪
Website:	**Bar/Restaurant rating:** ✪ ✪ ✪ ✪ ✪
Telephone:	**Staff rating:** ✪ ✪ ✪ ✪ ✪
Contacts:	
Email:	

	Par:
Shop: yes○ no○	**No. of holes:**
Telephone:	**Av. time complete round:**
Lessons: yes○ no○	**Green fees:**
Telephone:	
Carts for hire: yes○ no○	**Restaurant/bar:** yes○ no○
Practice range: yes○ no○	Telephone:
Practice greens: yes○ no○	*Comments*:

Comments:

COURSE REVIEW

Course name: **Address:** **Website:** **Telephone:** **Contacts:** **Email:**	**OVERALL RATING:** ✪ ✪ ✪ ✪ ✪ **Course rating:** ✪ ✪ ✪ ✪ ✪ **Shop rating:** ✪ ✪ ✪ ✪ ✪ **Bar/Restaurant rating:** ✪ ✪ ✪ ✪ ✪ **Staff rating:** ✪ ✪ ✪ ✪ ✪
Shop: yes○ no○ Telephone: **Lessons:** yes○ no○ Telephone: **Carts for hire:** yes○ no○ **Practice range:** yes○ no○ **Practice greens:** yes○ no○	**Par:** **No. of holes:** **Av. time complete round:** **Green fees:**
	Restaurant/bar: yes○ no○ Telephone: *Comments*:
Comments:	

COURSE REVIEW

Course name: **Address:** **Website:** **Telephone:** **Contacts:** **Email:**	**OVERALL RATING:** ✪ ✪ ✪ ✪ ✪ **Course rating:** ✪ ✪ ✪ ✪ ✪ **Shop rating:** ✪ ✪ ✪ ✪ ✪ **Bar/Restaurant rating:** ✪ ✪ ✪ ✪ ✪ **Staff rating:** ✪ ✪ ✪ ✪ ✪
Shop: yes○ no○ Telephone: **Lessons:** yes○ no○ Telephone: **Carts for hire:** yes○ no○ **Practice range:** yes○ no○ **Practice greens:** yes○ no○	**Par:** **No. of holes:** **Av. time complete round:** **Green fees:**
	Restaurant/bar: yes○ no○ Telephone: *Comments*:
Comments:	

COURSE REVIEW

Course name: **Address:** **Website:** **Telephone:** **Contacts:** **Email:**	**OVERALL RATING:** ✪ ✪ ✪ ✪ ✪ **Course rating:** ✪ ✪ ✪ ✪ ✪ **Shop rating:** ✪ ✪ ✪ ✪ ✪ **Bar/Restaurant rating:** ✪ ✪ ✪ ✪ ✪ **Staff rating:** ✪ ✪ ✪ ✪ ✪
Shop: yes◯ no◯ Telephone: **Lessons:** yes◯ no◯ Telephone: **Carts for hire:** yes◯ no◯ **Practice range:** yes◯ no◯ **Practice greens:** yes◯ no◯	**Par:** **No. of holes:** **Av. time complete round:** **Green fees:**
	Restaurant/bar: yes◯ no◯ Telephone: *Comments*:

Comments:

COURSE REVIEW

Course name: **Address:** **Website:** **Telephone:** **Contacts:** **Email:**	**OVERALL RATING:** ✪ ✪ ✪ ✪ ✪ **Course rating:** ✪ ✪ ✪ ✪ ✪ **Shop rating:** ✪ ✪ ✪ ✪ ✪ **Bar/Restaurant rating:** ✪ ✪ ✪ ✪ ✪ **Staff rating:** ✪ ✪ ✪ ✪ ✪
Shop: yes⃝ no⃝ Telephone: **Lessons:** yes⃝ no⃝ Telephone: **Carts for hire:** yes⃝ no⃝ **Practice range:** yes⃝ no⃝ **Practice greens:** yes⃝ no⃝	**Par:** **No. of holes:** **Av. time complete round:** **Green fees:**
	Restaurant/bar: yes⃝ no⃝ Telephone: *Comments*:

Comments:

Waterville (17th hole), Ireland

COURSE REVIEW

Course name: **Address:** **Website:** **Telephone:** **Contacts:** **Email:**	**OVERALL RATING:** ✪ ✪ ✪ ✪ ✪ **Course rating:** ✪ ✪ ✪ ✪ ✪ **Shop rating:** ✪ ✪ ✪ ✪ ✪ **Bar/Restaurant rating:** ✪ ✪ ✪ ✪ ✪ **Staff rating:** ✪ ✪ ✪ ✪ ✪
Shop: yes◯ no◯ Telephone: **Lessons:** yes◯ no◯ Telephone: **Carts for hire:** yes◯ no◯ **Practice range:** yes◯ no◯ **Practice greens:** yes◯ no◯	**Par:** **No. of holes:** **Av. time complete round:** **Green fees:**
	Restaurant/bar: yes◯ no◯ Telephone: *Comments*:

Comments:

COURSE REVIEW

Course name: **Address:** **Website:** **Telephone:** **Contacts:** **Email:**	**OVERALL RATING:** ✪ ✪ ✪ ✪ ✪ **Course rating:** ✪ ✪ ✪ ✪ ✪ **Shop rating:** ✪ ✪ ✪ ✪ ✪ **Bar/Restaurant rating:** ✪ ✪ ✪ ✪ ✪ **Staff rating:** ✪ ✪ ✪ ✪ ✪
Shop: yes○ no○ Telephone: **Lessons:** yes○ no○ Telephone: **Carts for hire:** yes○ no○ **Practice range:** yes○ no○ **Practice greens:** yes○ no○	**Par:** **No. of holes:** **Av. time complete round:** **Green fees:**
	Restaurant/bar: yes○ no○ Telephone: *Comments*:
Comments:	

COURSE REVIEW

Course name:
Address:

Website:
Telephone:
Contacts:
Email:

Shop: yes○ no○
Telephone:
Lessons: yes○ no○
Telephone:
Carts for hire: yes○ no○
Practice range: yes○ no○
Practice greens: yes○ no○

OVERALL RATING: ✪ ✪ ✪ ✪ ✪

Course rating: ✪ ✪ ✪ ✪ ✪
Shop rating: ✪ ✪ ✪ ✪ ✪
Bar/Restaurant rating: ✪ ✪ ✪ ✪ ✪
Staff rating: ✪ ✪ ✪ ✪ ✪

Par:
No. of holes:
Av. time complete round:
Green fees:

Restaurant/bar: yes○ no○
Telephone:
Comments:

Comments:

COURSE REVIEW

Course name: **Address:** **Website:** **Telephone:** **Contacts:** **Email:**	**OVERALL RATING:** ✪ ✪ ✪ ✪ ✪ **Course rating:** ✪ ✪ ✪ ✪ ✪ **Shop rating:** ✪ ✪ ✪ ✪ ✪ **Bar/Restaurant rating:** ✪ ✪ ✪ ✪ ✪ **Staff rating:** ✪ ✪ ✪ ✪ ✪
Shop: yes◯ no◯ Telephone: **Lessons:** yes◯ no◯ Telephone: **Carts for hire:** yes◯ no◯ **Practice range:** yes◯ no◯ **Practice greens:** yes◯ no◯	**Par:** **No. of holes:** **Av. time complete round:** **Green fees:**
	Restaurant/bar: yes◯ no◯ Telephone: *Comments*:

Comments:

Loch Lomond (9th hole), Scotland

TOP 100 GOLF COURSES CHECKLIST: BRITAIN AND IRELAND

Rank	Course (page references refer to photographs)	Location	Played
1	**Royal County Down** Newcastle, County Down, BT33 0AN, Northern Ireland +44 (0)28 4372 3314 www.royalcountydown.org	Northern Ireland	☐
2	**St Andrews (Old)** St. Andrews Links, St. Andrews, Fife, KY16 9SF Scotland +44 (0)1334 466666 www.standrews.org.uk *see page 131*	Scotland	☐
3	**Turnberry (Ailsa)** The Westin Turnberry Resort, Turnberry, Ayrshire, KA26 9LT, Scotland +44 (0)1655 334032 www.turnberry.co.uk *see pages 2–3*	Scotland	☐
4	**Muirfield** The Honourable Company of Edinburgh Golfers, Duncur Road, Gullane, East Lothian, EH31 2EG, Scotland +44 (0)1620 842123 www.muirfield.org.uk	Scotland	☐
5	**Royal Portrush (Dunluce)** Royal Portrush Golf Club, Dunluce Road, Co. Antrim, BT56 8JQ, Northern Ireland +44 (0)28 7082 2311 www.royalportrushgolfclub.com	Northern Ireland	☐
6	**Kingsbarns** Kingsbarns Golf Links, Kingsbarns, St. Andrews, Fife, KY16 8QD, Scotland +44 (0)1334 460860 www.kingsbarns.com *see pages 6–7 and page 126*	Scotland	☐
7	**Royal Birkdale** Royal Birkdale Golf Club, Waterloo Road, Birkdale, Southport, Merseyside PR8 2LX +44 (0)1704 567920 www.royalbirkdale.com	England	☐
8	**Carnoustie (Championship)** Carnoustie Golf Links, Links Parade, Carnoustie, Angus DD7 7JE, Scotland +44 (0)1241 853789 www.carnoustiegolflinks.co.uk	Scotland	☐
9	**Woodhall Spa (Hotchkin)** Woodhall Spa Golf Club, The Broadway, Woodhall Spa, Lincs, LN10 6PU, England +44 (0)1526 352511 www.woodhallspagolf.com	England	☐
10	**Ballybunion (Old)** Ballybunion Golf Club, Sandhill Road, Ballybunion, County Kerry, Ireland +353 (0)68 27146 www.ballybuniongolfclub.ie *see page 25*	Ireland	☑

Rank	Course	Location	Played

11   **Royal Dornoch (Championship)**   Scotland
Royal Dornoch Golf Club, Dornoch,
Sutherland, IV23 3LW, Scotland
+44 (0)1862 810219 www.royaldornoch.com

12   **Lahinch (Old)**   Ireland ✓
Lahinch Golf Club, Lahinch, County Clare, Ireland
+353 (0)65 7081 103 www.lahinchgolf.com
see page 84

13   **Loch Lomond**   Scotland
Loch Lomond Golf Club, Rossdhu House, Luss,
Dunbartonshire, G83 8NT, Scotland
+44 (0)1436 655555 www.lochlomond.com
see pages 120–1

14   **Waterville**   Ireland ✓
Waterville Golf Links, Waterville, County Kerry, Ireland
+353 66 947 4102 www.watervillehouse.com
see page 114

15   **Portmarnock (Old)**   Ireland
Portmarnock Golf Club, Portmarnock, County Dublin,
Ireland +353 1 846 2968 www.portmarnock.com

16   **Royal Liverpool**   England
Royal Liverpool Golf Club, Meols Drive, Hoylake,
Wirral, Merseyside, CH47 4AL, England
+44 (0)151 632 3101 www.royal-liverpool-golf.com

17   **Royal St George's**   England
Royal St George's Golf Club, Sandwich,
Kent, CT13 9PB, England
+44 (0)1304 613090 www.royalstgeorges.com

18   **European Club**   Ireland ✓
The European Club, Brittas Bay, Co Wicklow, Ireland
+353 404 47415 www.theeuropeanclub.com

19   **Sunningdale (Old)**   England
Sunningdale Golf Club, Ridgemount Road,
Sunningdale, Berkshire, SL5 9RR, England
+44 (0)1344 621681 www.sunningdale-golfclub.co.uk

20   **Royal Lytham & St Anne's**   England
Royal Lytham & St Anne's Golf Club, Links Gate,
St Anne's on Sea, Lancs., FY8 3LQ, England
+44 (0)1253 724206 www.royallytham.org

21   **Ganton**   England
Ganton Golf Club, Ganton, North Yorkshire,
YO12 4PA, England
+44 (0)1994 710329 www.gantongolfclub.com

22   **Wentworth (West)**   England
The Wentworth Club, Virginia Water, Surrey,
GU25 4LS, England
+44 (0)1344 842201 www.wentworthclub.com

TOP 100 GOLF COURSES CHECKLIST

Rank	Course	Location	Played
23	**Walton Heath (Old)** Walton Heath Golf Club, Deans Lane, Walton on the Hill, Surrey, KT20 7TP, England +44 (0)1737 812380 www.whgc.co.uk *see page 79*	England	
24	**Royal Troon (Old)** Royal Troon Golf Club, Craigend Road, Troon, Ayrshire, KA10 6EP, Scotland +44 (0)1292 311555 www.royaltroon.com	Scotland	
25	**Cruden Bay** Cruden Bay Golf Club, Aulton Road, Cruden Bay, Aberdeenshire, AB42 0NN, Scotland +44 (0)1799 812285 www.crudenbaygolfclub.co.uk	Scotland	
26	**Royal Porthcawl** Royal Porthcawl Golf Club, Rest Bay, Porthcawl, Mid Glamorgan, CF36 3VW, Wales +44 (0)1656 782251 www.royalporthcawl.com *see page 146*	Wales	
27	**Gleneagles (King's)** Gleneagles Hotel, Auchterarder, Perthshire, PH3 1NF, Scotland +44 (0)1764 662231 www.gleneagles.com	Scotland	
28	**Prestwick** Prestwick Golf Club, 2 Links Road, Prestwick, Ayrshire, KA9 1QG, Scotland +44 (0)1292 671020 www.prestwickgc.co.uk	Scotland	
29	**Machrihanish** Machrihanish Golf Club, Machrihanish, Campbeltown, Argyll, PA28 6PT, Scotland +44 (0)1586 810213 www.machgolf.com	Scotland	
30	**Nairn** Nairn Golf Club, Seabank Road, Nairn, IV12 4HB, Scotland +44 (0)1667 453208 www.nairngolfclub.co.uk *see page 151*	Scotland	
31	**St George's Hill** St George's Hill Golf Club, Golf Club Road, St George's Hill, Weybridge, Surrey, KT13 0NL, England +44 (0)1932 847758 www.stgeorgeshillgolfclub.co.uk	England	
32	**North Berwick (West)** North Berwick Golf Club, Beach Road, North Berwick, East Lothian, EH39 4BB, Scotland +44 (0)1620 892135 www.northberwickgolfclub.com	Scotland	
33	**Royal Aberdeen (Balgownie)** Royal Aberdeen Golf Club, Balgownie Links, Bridge of Don, Aberdeen, AB23 8AT, Scotland +44 (0)1224 702571 www.royalaberdeengolf.com	Scotland	

Rank	Course	Location	Played
34	**Saunton (East)** Saunton Golf Club, Braunton, North Devon, EX33 1LG, England +44 (0)1271 812436 www.sauntongolf.co.uk	England	
35	**St Enodoc (Church)** St Enodoc Golf Club, Rock, Wadebridge, Cornwall, PL27 6LD, England +44 (0)1208 862200 www.st-enodoc.co.uk *see page 109*	England	
36	**Carne** Carne Golf Links, Carne, Belmullet, Co. Mayo, Ireland + 353 (0)97 82292 www.carnegolflinks.com	Ireland	
37	**Hillside** Hillside Golf Club, Hastings Road, Hillside, Southport, Merseyside, PR8 2LU, England +44 (0)1704 567169 www.hillside-golfclub.co.uk	England	
38	**Old Head** Old Head Golf Links, Kinsale, Cork, Ireland +353 (0)21 477 8444 www.oldheadgolflinks.com *see pages 32–33*	Ireland	✓
39	**Western Gailes** Western Gailes Golf Club, Gailes, Irvine, Ayrshire, KA11 5AE, Scotland +44 (0)1294 311649 www.westerngailes.com	Scotland	
40	**Silloth on Solway** Silloth on Solway Golf Club, The Club House, Silloth on Solway, Cumbria, CA7 4BL, England +44 (0)16973 31304 www.sillothgolfclub.co.uk	England	
41	**Doonbeg** Doonbeg Golf Club, Doonbeg, Co.Clare, Ireland +353 659 055 246 www.doonbeggolfclub.com	Ireland	
42	**Formby** Formby Golf Club, Golf Road, Formby, Merseyside, L37 1LQ, England +44 (0)1704 872164 www.formbygolfclub.co.uk	England	
43	**Swinley Forest** Swinley Forest Golf Club, Coronation Road, Ascot, Berkshire, SL5 9LE, England +44 (0)1344 620197	England	
44	**Royal West Norfolk** Royal West Norfolk Golf Club, Brancaster, Norfolk, PE31 8AX, England +44 (0)1485 210223	England	
45	**Sunningdale (New)** Sunningdale Golf Club, Ridgemount Road, Sunningdale, Berkshire, SL5 9RR, England +44 (0)1344 621681 www.sunningdale-golfclub.co.uk	England	

TOP 100 GOLF COURSES CHECKLIST

Rank	Course	Location	Played
46	**K Club (Palmer)** The K Club, Straffan, Co. Kildare, Ireland +353 (0)16017200 www.kclub.ie	Ireland	☑
47	**Tralee** Tralee Golf Club, West Barrow, Ardfert, Tralee, Co. Kerry, Ireland +353 (0)66 713 6379 www.traleegolfclub.com	Ireland	☐
48	**Mount Juliet** Mount Juliet Conrad, Thomastown, County Kilkenny, Ireland +353 (0)56 777 3064 www.mountjuliet.com	Ireland	☐
49	**Gullane (No.1)** Gullane Golf Club, Gullane, East Lothian, EH31 2BB, Scotland +44 (0)1620 842255 www.gullanegolfclub.com	Scotland	☐
50	**County Sligo (Championship)** County Sligo Golf Club, Rosses Point, County Sligo, Ireland +353 7191 77 134 www.countysligogolfclub.ie	Ireland	☐
51	**Druids Glen** Druids Glen Golf Resort, Newtownmountkennedy, Co.Wicklow, Ireland +353 (0)1287 3600 www.druidsglen.ie	Ireland	☐
52	**Gleneagles (Queen's)** Auchterarder, Perthshire, PH3 1NF, Scotland +44 (0)1764 662231 www.gleneagles.com	Scotland	☐
53	**Island** The Island Golf Club, Corballis, Donabate, Co. Dublin, Ireland +353 (0)1843 6205 www.theislandgolfclub.com	Ireland	☐

Kingsbarns (4th hole), Scotland

Rank	Course	Location	Played
54	**Royal St David's** Royal St David's Golf Club, Harlech, Gwynedd, LL46 2UB, Wales +44 (0)1766 780361 www.royalstdavids.co.uk	Wales	
55	**Wentworth (East)** Wentworth Club, Virginia Water, Surrey, GU25 4LS, England +44 (0)1344 842201 www.wentworthclub.com	England	
56	**Notts** Notts Golf Club, Hollinwell, Kirby-in-Ashfield, Nottinghamshire, NG17 7QR, England +44 (0)1623 753225 www.nottsgolfclub.co.uk	England	
57	**Ballyliffin (Glashedy)** Ballyliffin Golf Club, Ballyliffin, Inishowen, Co. Donegal, Ireland +353 (0)7493 76119 www.ballyliffingolfclub.com	Ireland	
58	**Berkshire (Red)** The Berkshire Golf Club, Swinley Road, Ascot, Berkshire, SL5 8AY, England +44 (0)1344 621495	England	
59	**Nefyn & District (Old)** Nefyn & District Golf Club, Morfa Nefyn, Pwllheli, Gwynedd, LL53 6DA, Wales +44 (0)1758 720966 www.nefyn-golf-club.com	Wales	
60	**Rosapenna (Old)** Rosapenna Golf Links, Downings, Letterkenny, Co Donegal, Ireland +353 (0)74 915 5301 www.rosapennagolflinks.ie	Ireland	
61	**Royal Cinque Ports** Royal Cinque Ports Golf Club, Golf Road, Deal, Kent, CT14 6RF, England +44 (0)1304 374007 www.royalcinqueports.com *see page 141*	England	
62	**Blairgowrie (Rosemount)** Blairgowrie Golf Club, Golf Course Road, Rosemount, Blairgowrie, Perthshire, PH10 6LG, Scotland +44 (0)1250 872622 www.theblairgowriegolfclub.co.uk	Scotland	
63	**Carton House (Montgomerie)** Carton House, Maynooth, Co. Kildare, Ireland +353 (0)1 505 2000 www.carton.ie	Ireland	
64	**County Louth** County Louth Golf Club, Baltray, Drogheda, County Louth, Ireland +353 (0)41 988 1530 www.countylouthgolfclub.com	Ireland	
65	**Pennard** Pennard Golf Club, 2 Southgate Road, Southgate, Swansea, SA3 2BT, Wales +44 (0)1792 233131 www.pennardgolfclub.com	Wales	

TOP 100 GOLF COURSES CHECKLIST

Rank	Course	Location	Played
66	**Rye (Old)** Rye Golf Club, Camber, Rye, East Sussex, TN31 7QS, England +44 (0)1797 225241 www.ryegolfclub.co.uk	England	
67	**Worplesdon** Worplesdon Golf Club, Woking, Surrey, GU22 0RA, England +44 (0)1483 472277 www.worplesdongc.co.uk	England	
68	**Enniscrone (Dunes)** Enniscrone Golf Club, Enniscrone, Co. Sligo, Ireland +353 96 36297 www.enniscronegolf.com	Ireland	
69	**Aberdovey** Aberdovey Golf Club, Tywyn Road, Aberdovey, Gwynedd, LL35 0RT, Wales +44 (0)1654 767493 www.aberdoveygolf.co.uk	Wales	
70	**Woburn (Duke's)** Woburn Golf Club, Little Brickhill, Milton Keynes, Bucks, MK17 9LJ, England +44 (0)1908 370756 http://golf.discoverwoburn.co.uk	England	
71	**West Sussex** West Sussex Golf Club, Golf Club Lane, Wiggonholt, Pulborough, West Sussex, RH20 2EN, England +44 (0)1798 872426 www.westsussexgolf.co.uk	England	
72	**Machrie** Machrie Hotel & Golf Links, Port Ellen, Isle of Islay, PA42 7AT, Scotland +44 (0)1496 302310 www.machrie.com	Scotland	
73	**Hunstanton** Hunstanton Golf Club, Golf Course Road, Old Hunstanton, Norfolk, PE36 6JQ, England +44 (0)1485 532811 www.hunstantongolfclub.com	England	
74	**Belfry (Brabazon)** The Belfry, Wishaw, North Warwickshire, B76 9PR, England +44 (0)1675 470301 www.thebelfry.com	England	
75	**Alwoodley** Alwoodley Golf Club, Wigton Lane, Leeds, LS17 8SA, England +44 (0)113 268 1680 www.alwoodley.co.uk	England	
76	**Hankley Common** Hankley Common Golf Club, Tilford, Farnham, Surrey, GU10 2DD, England +44 (0)1252 792493 www.hankley.co.uk	England	
77	**Bearwood Lakes** Bearwood Lakes Golf Club, Bearwood Road, Sindlesham, Nr. Wokingham, Berkshire, RG41 4SJ, England +44 (0)118 979 7900 www.bearwoodlakes.co.uk	England	

Rank	Course	Location	Played
78	**Woburn (Marquess)** Woburn Golf Club, Little Brickhill, Milton Keynes, Bucks, MK17 9LJ, England +44 (0)1908 370756 http://golf.discoverwoburn.co.uk	England	☐
79	**Grove** The Grove, Chandler's Cross, Hertfordshire, WD3 4TG, England +44 (0)1923 294266 www.thegrove.co.uk	England	☐
80	**Adare Manor** Adare Manor Hotel & Golf Resort, Adare, Co. Limerick, Ireland +353 (0)61 396566 www.adaremanor.ie	Ireland	☐
81	**Moortown** Moortown Golf Club, Harrogate Road, Leeds, LS17 7DB, England +44 (0)113 268 6521 www.moortown-gc.co.uk	England	☐
82	**Chart Hills** Chart Hills Golf Club, Weeks Lane, Biddenden, Kent, TN27 8JX, England +44 (0)1580 292222 www.charthills.co.uk	England	☐
83	**Aldeburgh** Aldeburgh Golf Club, Saxmundham Road, Aldeburgh, Suffolk, IP15 5PE, England +44 (0)1728 452890 www.aldeburghgolfclub.co.uk	England	☐
84	**Berkshire (Blue)** West Hill Golf Club, Bagshot Road, Brookwood, Surrey, GU24 0BH, England +44 (0)1483 474365 www.westhill-golfclub.co.uk	England	☐
85	**West Hill** West Hill Golf Club, Bagshot Road, Brookwood, Surrey, GU24 0BH, England +44 (0)1483 474365 www.westhill-golfclub.co.uk	England	☐
86	**Burnham & Berrow** Burnham & Berrow Golf Club, St. Christopher's Way, Burnham-on-Sea, Somerset, TA8 2PE, England +44 (0)1278 785760 www.burnhamandberrowgolfclub.co.uk	England	☐
87	**Woburn (Duchess)** Woburn Golf Club, Little Brickhill, Milton Keynes, Bucks, MK17 9LJ, England +44 (0)1908 370756 http://golf.discoverwoburn.co.uk	England	☐
88	**Addington** The Addington Golf Club, Shirley Church Road, Addington, Croydon, Surrey, CR0 5AB, England +44 (0)208 777 1055 www.addingtongolf.com	England	☐
89	**Murcar** Murcar Links Golf Club, Bridge of Don, Aberdeen, AB23 8BD, Scotland +44 (0)1224 704354 www.murcarlinks.com	Scotland	☐

TOP 100 GOLF COURSES CHECKLIST

Rank	Course	Location	Played
90	**Castlerock (Mussenden)** Castlerock Golf Club, 65 Circular Road, Castlerock, Co Londonderry, BT51 4TJ, Northern Ireland +44 (0)28 7084 8314 www.castlerockgc.co.uk	Northern Ireland	☐
91	**St Andrews (Torrance)** Fairmont St Andrews, St Andrews, Fife, KY16 8PN, Scotland +44 (0)1334 837000 www.fairmontgolf.com	Scotland	☐
92	**Trevose (Championship)** Trevose Golf & Country Club, Constantine Bay, Padstow, Cornwall, PL28 8JB, England +44 (0)1841 520208 www.trevose-gc.co.uk	England	☐
93	**Castletown** Castletown Golf Links Hotel, Fort Island, Derbyhaven, Isle of Man, IM9 1UA +44 (0)1624 822220 www.castletowngolflinks.co.uk	England	☐
94	**Walton Heath (New)** Walton Heath Golf Club, Deans Lane, Walton on the Hill, Surrey, KT20 7TP, England +44 (0)1737 812380 www.whgc.co.uk	England	☐
95	**Royal North Devon** Royal North Devon Golf Club, Golf Links Road, Westward Ho!, Devon, EX39 1HD, England +44 (0)1237 477598 www.royalnorthdevongolfclub.co.uk	England	☐
96	**Portstewart (Strand)** Portstewart Golf Club, Strand Road, Portstewart, County Londonderry, BT55 7PG, Northern Ireland +44 (0)28 70832015 www.portstewartgc.co.uk	Northern Ireland	☐
97	**St Andrews (New)** St Andrews Links, St Andrews, Fife, KY16 9SF, Scotland +44 (0)1334 466666 www.standrews.org.uk	Scotland	☐
98	**Lindrick** Lindrick Golf Club, Lindrick Common, Worksop, Notts, S81 8BH, England +44 (0)1909 475282 www.lindrickgolfclub.co.uk	England	☐
99	**Royal Ashdown Forest (Old)** Royal Ashdown Forest GC, Chapel Lane, Forest Row, East Sussex, RH18 5LR, England +44 (0)1342 822018 www.royalashdown.co.uk	England	☐
100	**Saunton (West)** Saunton Golf Club, Braunton, North Devon, EX33 1LG, England +44 (0)1271 812436 www.sauntongolf.co.uk	England	☐

St. Andrew's (Old), Hell Bunker, Scotland

TOP 100 GOLF COURSES CHECKLIST: NORTH AMERICA

This checklist includes Canada, the United States (including Hawaii) and the Caribbean and Mexico.

Rank	Course	Location	Played
1	**Pine Valley** Pine Valley Golf Club, Clementon, New Jersey (NJ) 08021, USA +1 856 309 3203	NJ/USA	☐
2	**Cypress Point** Cypress Point Club, 17 Mile Drive, Pebble Beach, California (CA) 93953, USA +1 831 624 6444	CA/USA	☐
3	**Augusta National** Augusta National Golf Club, 2604 Washington Rd, Augusta, Georgia (GA) 30904, USA +1 706 667 6000 www.masters.org	GA/USA	☐
4	**Shinnecock Hills** Shinnecock Hills Golf Club, 200 Tuckahoe Road, Southampton, New York (NY) 11968, USA +1 631 283 3525	NY/USA	☐
5	**Pebble Beach** Pebble Beach Resorts, 1700 17 Mile Drive, Pebble Beach, California (CA) 93953, USA +1 800 654 9300 www.pebblebeach.com	CA/USA	☐
6	**Oakmont** Oakmont Country Club, 1233 Hulton Rd, Oakmont, Pennsylvania (PA) 15139, USA +1 412 828 4653 www.oakmont-countryclub.org	PA/USA	☐
7	**Merion (East)** Merion Golf Club, 450 Ardmore Avenue, Ardmore, Pennsylvania (PA) 19003, USA +1 610 642 5600 www.meriongolfclub.com	PA/USA	☑
8	**Sand Hills** Sand Hills Golf Club, Highway 97, Mullen, Nebraska (NE) 69152, USA +1 308 546 2437	NE/USA	☐
9	**Pacific Dunes** Bandon Dunes Golf Resort, 57744 Round Lake Drive, Bandon, Oregon 97411, USA +1 541 347 4380 www.bandondunesgolf.com	OR/USA	☐
10	**National Golf Links of America** National Golf Links of America, Sebonac Inlet Road, Southampton, Long Island, New York (NY) 11968, USA +1 631 283 0559	NY/USA	☐
11	**Seminole** Seminole Golf Club, 901 Seminole Blvd, Juno Beach, Florida (FL) 33408, USA +1 561 626 0280	FL/USA	☐

Rank	Course	Location	Played
12	**Winged Foot (West)** Winged Foot Golf Club, Fennimore Rd, Mamaroneck, New York (NY) 10543, USA +1 914 381 5821 www.wfgc.org	NY/USA	✓
13	**Crystal Downs** Crystal Downs Country Club, 1286 Frankfort Highway, Frankfort, Michigan (MI) 49635, USA +1 231 352 7979	MI/USA	
14	**Pinehurst (No.2)** Pinehurst Resort, 1 Carolina Vista Drive, Village of Pinehurst, North Carolina 28374, USA +1 910 295 6811 www.pinehurst.com	NC/USA	
15	**Oakland Hills (South)** Oakland Hills Country Club, Bloomfield Hills, Michigan (MI) 48301, USA +1 248 433 0671 www.oaklandhillscc.com	MI/USA	
16	**Fishers Island** Fishers Island Club, Fishers Island, New York (NY) 06390, USA +1 631 788 7223 www.fishersislandclub.com	NY/USA	✓
17	**Country Club (Main)** The Country Club, 191 Clyde Street, Brookline, Massachusetts (MA) 01246, USA +1 617 566 0240 www.tcclub.org	MA/USA	
18	**Prairie Dunes** Prairie Dunes Country Club, 4812 E 30th Ave, Hutchinson, Kansas (KS) 67502, USA +1 620 662 0581 www.prairiedunes.com	KS/USA	
19	**Chicago** Chicago Golf Club, Warrenville Rd, Wheaton, Illinois (IL) 60187, USA +1 630 665 2988	IL/USA	
20	**Bethpage (Black)** Bethpage State Park, Farmingdale, New York (NY) 11735, USA +1 516 249 0700 http://nysparks.state.ny.us/golf/info.asp?golfID=12	NY/USA	
21	**Muirfield Village** Muirfield Village Golf Club, 5750 Memorial Drive, Dublin, Ohio (OH) 43017, USA +1 614 889 6740 www.muirfieldvillage.com	OH/USA	
22	**San Francisco** San Francisco Golf Club, Junipero Serra Blvd, San Francisco, California (CA) 94132, USA +1 415 469 4122	CA/USA	
23	**Whistling Straits (Straits)** Whistling Straits, 444 Highland Drive, Kohler, Wisconsin (WI) 53044, USA +1 800 618 5535 www.whistlingstraits.com	WI/USA	

TOP 100 GOLF COURSES CHECKLIST

Rank	Course	Location	Played
24	**Olympic Club (Lake)** Olympic Club, 599 Skyline Blvd, San Francisco, California (CA) 94132, USA +1 415 587 8338 www.olyclub.com	CA/USA	☐
25	**Medinah (No.3)** Medinah Country Club, Medinah Rd, Medinah, Illinois (IL) 60157, USA +1 630 773 1700 www.medinahcc.org	IL/USA	☐
26	**Oak Hill (East)** Oak Hill Country Club, 346 Kilbourn Rd, Rochester, New York (NY) 14618, USA +1 585 586 1660 www.oakhillcc.com	NY/USA	☐
27	**Los Angeles (North)** 10101 Wilshire Blvd, Los Angeles, California (CA) 90024, USA +1 310 276 6104	CA/USA	☐
28	**Southern Hills** Southern Hills Country Club, 2636 East 61st Street, Tulsa, Oklahoma (OK) 74136, USA +1 918 492 3351 www.southernhillscc.com	OK/USA	☐
29	**Kiawah Island (Ocean)** Kiawah Island Golf Resort, 1 Sanctuary Beach Drive, Kiawah Island, South Carolina 29455, USA +1 843 768 2121 www.kiawahresort.com	SC/USA	☐
30	**Bandon Dunes** Bandon Dunes Golf Resort, 57744 Round Lake Drive, Bandon, Oregon 97411, USA +1 541 347 4380 www.bandondunesgolf.com	OR/USA	☐
31	**Riviera** Riviera Country Club, 1250 Capri Drive, Pacific Palisades, California (CA) 90272, USA +1 310 454 6591 www.therivieracountryclub.com	CA/USA	☐
32	**Baltusrol (Lower)** 201 Shunpike Road, Springfield, New Jersey (NJ) 07081, USA +1 973 376 1900 www.baltusrol.org	NJ/USA	☐
33	**Quaker Ridge** Griffen Avenue, Scarsdale, New York (NY) 10583, USA +1 914 725 1100 www.quakerridgegc.org	NY/USA	☐
34	**Golf Club** The Golf Club, 4522 Kitzmiller Rd, New Albany, Ohio (OH) 43054, USA +1 614 855 7326	OH/USA	☐
35	**Winged Foot (East)** Winged Foot Golf Club, Fennimore Rd, Mamaroneck, New York (NY) 10543, USA +1 914 381 5821 www.wfgc.org	NY/USA	☐

Rank	Course	Location	Played
36	**Garden City** Garden City Golf Club, 315 Stewart Ave, Garden City, New York (NY) 11530, USA +1 516 746 8360	NY/USA	
37	**Inverness** 4601 Dorr Street, Toledo, Ohio (OH) 43615, USA +1 419 578 9000 www.invernessclub.com	OH/USA	
38	**Cabo del Sol (Ocean)** Cabo del Sol Resort, 7 5 Carretera Transpeninsular, San Jose Del Cabo 23400, Mexico +1 800 386 2465 www.cabodelsol.com	Mexico	
39	**Highland Links** Ingonish Beach, Nova Scotia, B0C 1L0, Canada +1 800 441 1118 www.highlandslinksgolf.com	Canada	
40	**Shadow Creek (North)** Shadow Creek, 3 Shadow Creek Drive, North Las Vegas, Nevada (NV) 89031, USA +1 866 260 0069 www.shadowcreek.com	NV/USA	
41	**St George's** 1668 Islington Avenue, Etobicoke, Ontario M9A 3M9, Canada +1 416 231 3393 www.stgeorges.org	Canada	
42	**Camargo** The Camargo Club, 8605 Shawnee Run Road, Cincinnati, Ohio (OH) 45243, USA +1 (0)513 561 7213	OH/USA	
43	**Hamilton (West & South)** Hamilton Golf & Country Club, 232 Golf Links Road, Ancaster, Ontario L9G 2N5, Canada +1 905 648 4471 www.hgcc.ca	Canada	
44	**Spyglass Hill** Spyglass Hill Rd, Pebble Beach, California (CA) 93953, USA +1 831 625 8563 www.pebblebeach.com	CA/USA	
45	**Scioto** Scioto Country Club, 2196 Riverside Drive, Columbus, Ohio (OH) 43221, USA +1 614 486 4341 www.sciotocc.com	OH/USA	
46	**Somerset Hills** 180 Mine Mount Rd, Bernardsville, New Jersey (NJ) 07924, USA +1 908 766 0044	NJ/USA	
47	**Congressional (Blue)** 8500 River Rd, Bethesda, Maryland (MD) 20817, USA +1 (0)301 469 2032 www.ccclub.org	MD/USA	
48	**East Lake** East Lake Golf Club, 2575 Alston Drive, Atlanta, Georgia (GA) 30317, USA +1 404 373 5722 www.eastlakegolfclub.com	GA/USA	

TOP 100 GOLF COURSES CHECKLIST

Rank	Course	Location	Played
49	**Maidstone** Old Beach Lane, East Hampton, New York (NY) 11937, USA +1 516 324 5530	NY/USA	☐
50	**Harbour Town** Harbour Town Golf Links, The Sea Pines Resort, 32 Greenwood Dr, Hilton Head Island, South Carolina (SC) 29928, USA +1 800 925 4653 www.seapines.com	SC/USA	☐
51	**Shoreacres** 1601 Shore Acres Rd, Lake Bluff, Illinois (IL) 60044, USA +1 847 234 1472	IL/USA	☐
52	**Nanea** Nanea Golf Club, 75-1027 Henry St, Kailua Kona, Hawaii (HI) 96740, USA +1 (0)808 930 1300	Hawaii/USA	☐
53	**Old Sandwich** Old Sandwich Golf Club, 44 Talcott Pines Rd, Plymouth, Massachusetts (MA) 2541, USA +1 (0)508 209 2270	MA/USA	☐
54	**Ballyneal** Ballyneal, 216 South Interocean Avenue, Holyoke, Colorado (CO) 80734, USA +1 (0)970 854 5900 www.ballyneal.com	CO/USA	☐

San Roque (Old), 2nd hole, Spain

Rank	Course	Location	Played
55	**Wade Hampton** Hwy 107 South, Cashiers, North Carolina (NC) 28717, USA +1 828 743 5950 www.wadehamptongc.com	NC/USA	
56	**Butler National** Butler National Golf Club, 2616 York Rd, Oak Brook, Illinois (IL) 60523, USA +1 (0)630 990 3333	IL/USA	
57	**Victoria National** 2000 Victoria National Boulevard, Newburgh, Indiana (IN) 47630, USA +1 812 858 8230 www.victorianational.com	IN/USA	
58	**Kinloch** Kinloch Golf Club, 1100 Hockett Rd, Manakin-Sabot, Virginia (VA) 23103, USA +1 804 784 8000 www.kinlochclub.com	VA/USA	
59	**Friar's Head** Friar's Head, 2850 Sound Ave, Riverhead, New York (NY) 11901, USA +1(0)631 722 5200 www.friarshead.org	NY/USA	
60	**National Golf Club of Canada** National Golf Club of Canada, 134 Club House Dr, Woodbridge, Ontario L4L 2W2, Canada +1 905 851 7422	Canada	
61	**Honors Course** 9603 Lee Highway, Ooltewah, Tennessee (TN) 37363, USA +1 423 238 4272 www.honorscourse.net	TN/USA	
62	**Castle Pines** 1000 Hummingbird Lane, Castle Rock, Colorado (CO) 80104, USA +1 303 688 6000	CO/USA	
63	**Princeville (Prince)** Princeville at Hanalei, 5520 Ka Haku Road, Princeville, Kauai, Hawaii (HI) 96722-3069, USA +1 808 826 5000 www.princeville.com	HI/USA	
64	**Olympia Fields (North)** Olympia Fields Country Club, 2800 Country Club Drive, Olympia Fields, Illinois (IL) 60461, USA +1 708 748 0495 www.ofcc.info	IL/USA	
65	**Forest Highlands (Canyon)** 657 Forest Highlands Drive, Flagstaff, Arizona (AZ) 86001, USA +1 (0)520 525 9014 www.fhgc.com	AZ/USA	
66	**Arcadia Bluffs** Arcadia Bluffs, 14710 Northwood Highway, Arcadia, Michigan (MI) 49613, USA +1 231 889 3001 www.arcadiabluffs.com	MI/USA	

TOP 100 GOLF COURSES CHECKLIST

Rank	Course	Location	Played
67	**Quarry at La Quinta** 1 Quarry Lane, La Quinta, California (CA) 92253, USA +1 760 777 1100 www.quarryinfo.com	CA/USA	☐
68	**Milwaukee** 8000 N Range Line Rd, River Hills, Wisconsin (WI) 53217, USA +1 (0)414 362 5252	WI/USA	☐
69	**Mid Ocean Club** Hamilton, HM GX, Bermuda +1 441 293 0330 www.themidoceanclubbermuda.com	Bermuda	✓
70	**Flint Hills National** 1 Flint Hills National Drive, Andover, Kansas (KS) 67002, USA +1 316 733 7272 www.flinthillsnational.com	KS/USA	☐
71	**Shoal Creek** 100 New Williamsburg Drive, Birmingham, Alabama (AL) 35242, USA +1 205 991 9001 www.shoal-creek.com/shoalcreekclub	AL/USA	☐
72	**Rich Harvest Links** Rich Harvest Links, Dugan Road, Sugar Grove, Illinois (IL) 60554, USA +1 630 466 7610	IL/USA	☐
73	**Beacon Hall** Beacon Hall, 400 Beacon Hall Drive, Aurora, Ontario, L4G 3G8, Canada +1 905 841 9070 www.beaconhall.com	Canada	☐
74	**Cherry Hills** 4125 S. University Boulevard, Cherry Hills Village, Colorado (CO) 80113, USA +1 303 761 9900	CO/USA	☐
75	**Capilano** Capilano Golf & Country Club, 420 Southborough Drive, West Vancouver BC, V7S 1M2, Canada +1 604 922-9331 www.capilanogolf.com	Canada	☐
76	**Kittansett** Kittansett Club, 11 Point Rd, Marion, Massachusetts (MA) 02738, USA +1 508 748 0192 www.kittansett.org	MA/USA	☐
77	**TPC at Sawgrass (Stadium)** Tournament Players Club Sawgrass, 110 TPC Blvd, Ponte Vedra Beach, Florida (FL) 32082, USA +1 904 273 3230 www.tpc.com/daily/sawgrass/index.html	FL/USA	☐
78	**Dallas National** Dallas National Golf Club, 1515 Knoxville Street, Dallas, Texas 75211, USA +1 214 331 6144 www.dallasnationalgolfclub.com	TX/USA	☐

Rank	Course	Location	Played
79	**Sand Ridge** Sand Ridge Golf Club, 12150 Mayfield Road, Chardon, Ohio (OH) 44024, USA +1 440 285 8088 www.sandridgegolf.com	OH/USA	
80	**Interlachen** 6200 Interlachen Blvd, Edina, Minnesota (MN) 55436 USA +1 612 924 7424 www.interlachencc.org	MN/USA	
81	**Shaughnessy** Shaughnessy Golf & CC, 4300 S.W. Marine Drive, Vancouver<British Columbia, V6N 4A6, Canada +1 604 266 4141 www.shaughnessy.org	Canada	
82	**Lost Dunes** Lost Dunes Golf Club, 9300 Red Arrow Highway, Bridgman, Michigan (MI) 49106, USA +1 (0) 269 465 9300 www.lostdunes.com	MI/USA	
83	**Eugene** Eugene Country Club, 255 Country Club Rd, Eugene, Oregon (OR) 97401, USA +1 (0) 541 344 5124 www.eugenecountryclub.com	OR/USA	
84	**Grandfather** Grandfather Golf & Country Club, 2120 Highway 105 Linville, North Carolina (NC) 28646, USA +1 (0) 828 898 4531 www.grandfatherclub.org	NC/USA	
85	**Mayacama** Mayacama Golf Club, 525 Mayacama Club Drive, Santa Rosa, California (CA) 95403, USA +1 707-569-2900 www.mayacama.com	CA/USA	
86	**Black Diamond Ranch (Quarry)** 2600 W Black Diamond Cir, Lecanto, Florida (FL) 34461, USA +1 352 746 3446 www.blackdiamondranch.com	FL/USA	✓
87	**Valhalla** Valhalla Golf Club, 15503 Shelbyville Road, Louisville, Kentucky (KY) 40245, USA +1 502 245 1239	KY/USA	
88	**Blackwolf Run (River)** 1111 W Riverside Drive, Kohler, Wisconsin (WI) 53044, USA +1 920 457 4446 www.destinationkohler.com	WI/USA	
89	**Redtail** Redtail Golf Course, Rural Route 2, Port Stanley, Ontario, N5L 1J2, Canada +1 519 633 4653 www.redtailgolf.ca	Canada	
90	**Double Eagle** 6025 Cheshire Rd, Galena, Ohio (OH) 43021, USA +1 740 548 5454	OH/USA	

TOP 100 GOLF COURSES CHECKLIST

Rank	Course	Location	Played
91	**Royal Montreal (Blue)** Royal Montreal Golf Club, 25 South Ridge, Ile Bizard, Quebec, H9E 1B3, Canada +1 514 626 3977 www.rmgc.org	Canada	
92	**Ocean Forest** Ocean Forest Golf Club, 200 Ocean Rd, Sea Island, Georgia (GA) 31561, USA +1 912 638 5835	GA/USA	
93	**Punta Espada** Punta Espada Golf Club, Cap Cana, Punta Cana, Dominican Republic +1 809 472 2525 www.capcana.com	Dominican Republic	
94	**Banff Springs** Banff Springs Golf Club, 405 Spray Avenue, Banff, Alberta, T0L 0C0, Canada www.banffspringsgolfclub.com	Canada	
95	**El Dorado** Cabo San Lucas, Los Cabos, Baja California Sur, Mexico, 23410 +52 114 4 0040	Mexico	
96	**Links at Crowbush Cove** Links at Crowbush Cove, Lakeside Route 350, Morell, Prince Edward Island, C0A 1S0, Canada +1 902 368 5761 http://golflinkspei.com	Canada	
97	**Abaco Club** Abaco Club on Winding Bay, Marsh Harbour, Great Abaco Island, The Bahamas +1 242 367 0077 www.theabacoclub.com	The Bahamas	
98	**Jasper Park Lodge** Jasper Park Lodge, Old Lodge Road, Jasper, Alberta, T0E 1E0, Canada +1 780 852 3301 www.jasperparklodge.com	Canada	
99	**Great Exuma at Emerald Bay** Four Seasons Great Exuma, Queen's Highway, Emerald Bay, Great Exuma, The Bahamas +1 242 336 6800 www.fourseasons.com/greatexuma/	The Bahamas	
100	**Glen Abbey** Glen Abbey Golf Club, 1333 Dorval Drive, Oakville, Ontario, L6J 4Z3, Canada +1 905 844 1811 www.glenabbey.com	Canada	

Royal Cinque Ports, England

TOP 100 GOLF COURSES CHECKLIST: THE WORLD

Rank	Course	Location	Played
1	**Pine Valley** Pine Valley Golf Club, Clementon, New Jersey (NJ) 08021, USA +1 856 309 3203	USA	☐
2	**Royal County Down** Royal County Down Golf Club, Newcastle, County Down, BT33 0AN, Northern Ireland +44 (0)28 4372 3314 www.royalcountydown.org	Northern Ireland	☐
3	**Cypress Point** Cypress Point Club, 17 Mile Drive, Pebble Beach, California (CA) 93953, USA +1 831 624 6444	USA	☐
4	**St Andrews (Old)** St Andrews Links, Pilmour House, St Andrews, Fife, KY16 9SF, Scotland +44 (0)1334 466666 www.standrews.org.uk *see page 131*	Scotland	☐
5	**Augusta National** Augusta National Golf Club, 2604 Washington Rd, Augusta, Georgia (GA) 30904, USA +1 706 667 6000 www.masters.org/en_US/index.html	USA	☐
6	**Shinnecock Hills** Shinnecock Hills Golf Club, 200 Tuckahoe Road, Southampton, New York (NY) 11968, USA +1 631 283 3525	USA	☐
7	**Pebble Beach** Pebble Beach Resorts, 1700 17 Mile Drive, Pebble Beach, California (CA) 93953, USA +1 800 654 9300 www.pebblebeach.com	USA	☐
8	**Oakmont** Oakmont Country Club, 1233 Hulton Rd, Oakmont, Pennsylvania (PA) 15139, USA +1 412 828 4653 www.oakmont-countryclub.org	USA	☐
9	**Merion (East)** Merion Golf Club, 450 Ardmore Avenue, Ardmore, Pennsylvania (PA) 19003, USA +1 610 642 5600 www.meriongolfclub.com	USA	☐
10	**Sand Hills** Sand Hills Golf Club, Highway 97, Mullen, Nebraska (NE) 69152, USA +1 308 546 2437	USA	☐
11	**Turnberry (Ailsa)** Westin Turnberry Resort, Turnberry, Ayrshire, KA26 9LT, Scotland +44 (0)1655 334032 www.turnberry.co.uk *see pages 2–3*	Scotland	☐

Rank	Course	Location	Played
12	**Muirfield** Honourable Company of Edinburgh Golfers, Duncur Road, Gullane, East Lothian, EH31 2EG, Scotland +44 (0)1620 842123 www.muirfield.org.uk	Scotland	
13	**Royal Portrush (Dunluce)** Royal Portrush Golf Club, Dunluce Road, County Antrim, BT56 8JQ, Northern Ireland +44 (0)28 7082 2311 www.royalportrushgolfclub.com	Northern Ireland	
14	**Royal Melbourne (West)** Cheltenham Road, Black Rock, Victoria, 3193, Australia +61 3 9598 6755 www.royalmelbourne.com.au	Australia	
15	**Kingsbarns** Kingsbarns Golf Links, Kingsbarns, St Andrews, Fife, KY16 8QD, Scotland +44 (0)1334 460860 www.kingsbarns.com *see pages 6–7 and page 126*	Scotland	
16	**Royal Birkdale** Royal Birkdale Golf Club, Waterloo Road, Birkdale, Southport, Merseyside, PR8 2LX, England +44 (0)1704 567920 www.royalbirkdale.com	England	
17	**Carnoustie (Championship)** Carnoustie Golf Links, Links Parade, Carnoustie, Angus, DD7 7JE, Scotland +44 (0)1241 853789 www.carnoustiegolflinks.co.uk	Scotland	
18	**Woodhall Spa (Hotchkin)** Woodhall Spa Golf Club, The Broadway, Woodhall Spa, Lincs, LN10 6PU, England +44 (0)1526 352511 www.woodhallspagolf.com	England	
19	**Ballybunion (Old)** Ballybunion Golf Club, Sandhill Road, Ballybunion, County Kerry, Ireland +353 (0)68 27146 www.ballybuniongolfclub.ie *see page 25*	Ireland	
20	**Royal Dornoch (Championship)** Royal Dornoch Golf Club, Golf Road, Dornoch, Sutherland, IV25 3LW, Scotland +44 (0)1862 810219 www.royaldornoch.com	Scotland	
21	**Pacific Dunes** Bandon Dunes Golf Resort, 57744 Round Lake Drive, Bandon, Oregon 97411, USA +1 541 347 4380 www.bandondunesgolf.com	USA	
22	**National Golf Links of America** National Golf Links of America, Sebonac Inlet Road, Southampton, Long Island, New York (NY) 11968, USA +1 631 283 0559	USA	
23	**Seminole** Seminole Golf Club, 901 Seminole Blvd, Juno Beach, Florida (FL) 33408, USA +1 561 626 0280	USA	

TOP 100 GOLF COURSES CHECKLIST

Rank	Course	Location	Played
24	**Winged Foot (West)** Winged Foot Golf Club, Fennimore Rd, Mamaroneck, New York (NY) 10543, USA +1 914 381 5821 www.wfgc.org	USA	☐
25	**Crystal Downs** Crystal Downs Country Club, 1286 Frankfort Highway, Frankfort, Michigan (MI) 49635, USA +1 231 352 7979	USA	☐
26	**Pinehurst (No.2)** Pinehurst Resort, 1 Carolina Vista Drive, Village of Pinehurst, North Carolina 28374, USA +1 910 295 6811 www.pinehurst.com	USA	☐
27	**Kingston Heath** Kingston Heath Golf Club, Kingston Road, Cheltenham, Victoria 3192, Australia +61 (0)3 9551 1955 www.kingstonheath.com.au	Australia	☐
28	**Oakland Hills (South)** Oakland Hills Country Club, Bloomfield Hills, Michigan (MI) 48301, USA +1 248 433 0671 www.oaklandhillscc.com	USA	☐
29	**Fishers Island** Fishers Island Club, Fishers Island, New York (NY) 06390, USA +1 631 788 7223 www.fishersislandclub.com	USA	☐
30	**New South Wales** NSW Golf Club, Henry Head, Botany Bay National Park, La Perouse, NSW 2036, Australia +61 (0)2 9661 4455 www.nswgolfclub.com.au	Australia	☐
31	**Cape Kidnappers** Cape Kidnappers, 448 Clifton Road, Te Awagna, Hawke's Bay, New Zealand +64 (0) 6 873 0141 www.capekidnappers.com	New Zealand	☐
32	**Country Club (Main)** The Country Club, 191 Clyde Street, Brookline, Massachusetts (MA) 01246, USA +1 617 566 0240 www.countryclub.at	USA	☐
33	**Prairie Dunes** Prairie Dunes Country Club, 4812 E 30th Ave, Hutchinson, Kansas (KS) 67502, USA +1 620 662 0581 www.prairiedunes.com	USA	☐
34	**Chicago** Chicago Golf Club, Warrenville Rd, Wheaton, Illinois (IL) 60187, USA +1 630 665 2988	USA	☐
35	**Hirono** Hirono Golf Club, Shijimi, Hyogo, Kinki, Honshu, Japan +81 794 85 0123	Japan	☐

Rank	Course	Location	Played

36 **Bethpage (Black)**
Bethpage State Park, Farmingdale,
New York (NY) 11735, USA
+1 516 249 0700 http://nysparks.state.ny.us/golf/info.asp?golfID=12
USA

37 **Morfontaine**
Golf de Morfontaine, Mortefontaine 60128, France
+33 (0)3 44 54 68 27
France

38 **Muirfield Village**
Muirfield Village Golf Club, 5750 Memorial Drive,
Dublin, Ohio (OH) 43017, USA
+1 614 889 6740 www.muirfieldvillage.com
USA

39 **San Francisco**
San Francisco Golf Club, Junipero Serra Blvd,
San Francisco, California (CA) 94132, USA
+1 415 469 4122
USA

40 **Casa de Campo (Teeth of the Dog)**
Casa de Campo, La Romana, Dominican Republic
+1 809 523 3333 www.casadecampo.com.do
Dominican Republic

41 **Whistling Straits (Straits)**
Whistling Straits, 444 Highland Drive, Kohler,
Wisconsin (WI) 53044, USA
+1 800 618 5535 www.whistlingstraits.com
USA

42 **Lahinch (Old)**
Lahinch Golf Club, Lahinch, County Clare, Ireland
+353 065 7081003 www.lahinchgolf.com
see page 184
Ireland

43 **Olympic Club (Lake)**
Olympic Club, 599 Skyline Blvd, San Francisco,
California (CA) 94132, USA
+1 415 587 8338 www.olyclub.com
USA

44 **Medinah (No.3)**
Medinah Country Club, Medinah Rd,
Medinah, Illinois (IL) 60157, USA
+1 630 773 1700 www.medinahcc.org
USA

45 **Loch Lomond**
Loch Lomond Golf Club, Rossdhu House,
Luss, Dunbartonshire, G83 8NT, Scotland
+44 (0)1436 655555 www.lochlomond.com
see pages 120–121
Scotland

46 **Oak Hill (East)**
Oak Hill Country Club, 346 Kilbourn Rd, Rochester,
New York (NY) 14618, USA
+1 585 586 1660 www.oakhillcc.com
USA

47 **Waterville**
Waterville Golf Links, Waterville, County Kerry, Ireland
+353 66 947 4102 www.watervillehouse.com
see page 114
Ireland

TOP 100 GOLF COURSES CHECKLIST

Rank	Course	Location	Played
48	**Portmarnock (Old)** Portmarnock Golf Club, Portmarnock, County Dublin, Ireland +353 1 846 2968 www.portmarnockgolfclub.ie	Ireland	☐
49	**Royal Liverpool** Royal Liverpool Golf Club, Meols Drive, Hoylake, Wirral, Merseyside, CH47 4AL, England +44 (0)151 632 3101 www.royal-liverpool-golf.com	England	☐
50	**Royal St George's** Royal St George's Golf Club, Sandwich, Kent, CT13 9PB, England +44 (0)1304 613090 www.royalstgeorges.com	England	☐
51	**European Club** The European Club, Brittas Bay, Co Wicklow, Ireland +353 404 47415 www.theeuropeanclub.com	Ireland	☐
52	**Sunningdale (Old)** Sunningdale Golf Club, Ridgemount Road, Sunningdale, Berkshire, SL5 9RR, England +44 (0)1344 621681 www.sunningdale-golfclub.co.uk	England	☐
53	**Los Angeles (North)** 10101 Wilshire Blvd, Los Angeles, California (CA) 90024, USA +1 310 276 6104	USA	☐

Royal Porthcawl (2nd hole), Wales

Rank	Course	Location	Played
54	**Southern Hills** Southern Hills Country Club, 2636 East 61st Street, Tulsa, Oklahoma (OK) 74136, USA +1 918 492 3351 www.southernhillscc.com	USA	☐
55	**Kiawah Island (Ocean)** Kiawah Island Golf Resort, 1 Sanctuary Beach Drive, Kiawah Island, South Carolina 29455, USA +1 843 768 2121 www.kiawahresort.com	USA	☐
56	**Royal Lytham & St Anne's** Royal Lytham & St Anne's Golf Club, Links Gate, St Anne's on Sea, Lancs., FY8 3LQ, England +44 (0)1253 724206 www.royallytham.org	England	☐
57	**Bandon Dunes** Bandon Dunes Golf Resort, 57744 Round Lake Drive, Bandon, Oregon 97411, USA +1 541 347 4380 www.bandondunesgolf.com	USA	☐
58	**Riviera** Riviera Country Club, 1250 Capri Drive, Pacific Palisades, California (CA) 90272, USA +1 310 454 6591 www.therivieracountryclub.com	USA	☐
59	**Barnbougle Dunes** Barnbougle Dunes, 426 Waterhouse Road, Bridport, Tasmania 7262, Australia +61 (0) 363 560 094 www.barnbougledunes.com	Australia	☐
60	**Kauri Cliffs** Matauri Bay Road, Matauri Bay, Northland, New Zealand +64 (0)9 407 0060 www.kauricliffs.com	New Zealand	☐
61	**Baltusrol (Lower)** 201 Shunpike Road, Springfield, New Jersey (NJ) 07081, USA +1 973 376 1900 www.baltusrol.org	USA	☐
62	**Quaker Ridge** Griffen Avenue, Scarsdale, New York (NY) 10583, USA +1 914 725 1100 www.quakerridgegc.org	USA	☐
63	**Ganton** Ganton Golf Club, Ganton, North Yorkshire, YO12 4PA, England +44 (0) 1994 710329 www.gantongolfclub.com	England	☐
64	**Golf Club** The Golf Club, 4522 Kitzmiller Rd, New Albany, Ohio (OH) 43054, USA +1 614 855 7326	USA	☐
65	**Nine Bridges** Nine Bridges Resort, Kwangpyong-ri, Anduk-myon, South Jeju-gun, Jeju Island, South Korea +82 64 793 9999 www.ninebridges.co.kr	South Korea	☐

TOP 100 GOLF COURSES CHECKLIST

Rank	Course	Location	Played
66	**Winged Foot (East)** Winged Foot Golf Club, Fennimore Rd, Mamaroneck, New York (NY) 10543, USA +1 914 381 5821 www.wfgc.org	USA	
67	**Garden City** Garden City Golf Club, 315 Stewart Ave, Garden City, New York (NY) 11530, USA +1 516 746 8360	USA	
68	**Wentworth (West)** The Wentworth Club, Virginia Water, Surrey, GU25 4LS, England +44 (0)1344 842201 www.wentworthclub.com	England	
69	**Walton Heath (Old)** Walton Heath Golf Club, Deans Lane, Walton on the Hill, Surrey, KT20 7TP, England +44 (0)1737 812380 www.whgc.co.uk *See page 79*	England	
70	**Inverness** 4601 Dorr Street, Toledo, Ohio (OH) 43615, USA +1 419 578 9000 www.invernessclub.com	USA	
71	**Royal Troon (Old)** Royal Troon Golf Club, Craigend Road, Troon, Ayrshire, KA10 6EP, Scotland +44 (0)1292 311555 www.royaltroon.com	Scotland	
72	**Cruden Bay** Cruden Bay Golf Club, Aulton Road, Cruden Bay, Aberdeenshire, AB42 0NN, Scotland +44 (0)1799 812285 www.crudenbaygolfclub.co.uk	Scotland	
73	**Cabo del Sol (Ocean)** Cabo del Sol Resort, 7 5 Carretera Transpeninsular, San Jose Del Cabo 23400, Mexico +1 800 386 2465 www.cabodelsol.com	Mexico	
74 I	**Highland Links** Ingonish Beach, Nova Scotia, B0C 1L0, Canada +1 800 441 1118 www.highlandslinksgolf.com	Canada	
75	**Shadow Creek (North)** Shadow Creek, 3 Shadow Creek Drive, North Las Vegas, Nevada (NV) 89031, USA +1 866 260 0069 www.shadowcreek.com	USA	
76	**St George's** 1668 Islington Avenue, Etobicoke, Ontario M9A 3M9, Canada +1 416 231 3393 www.stgeorges.org	Canada	
77	**Kawana (Fuji)** 1459 Kawana, Ito City, Shizuoka, Chubu, Honshu, Japan +81 557 45 1111 www.princehotels.co.jp/kawana/	Japan	
78	**Tokyo** 1984 Kashiwabara, Sayama City, Saitama, Kanto, Honshu, Japan +81 429 53 9111	Japan	

Rank	Course	Location	Played
79	**Royal Adelaide** Royal Adelaide Golf Club, 328 Tapleys Hill Road, Seaton, Adelaide, South Australia 5023, Australia +61 (0)883 565 511 www.royaladelaidegolf.com.au	Australia	
80	**Camargo** The Camargo Club, 8605 Shawnee Run Road, Cincinnati, Ohio (OH) 45243, USA +1 (0)513 561 7213	USA	
81	**Valderrama** Club de Golf Valderrama, 11310 Sotogrande, Prov de Cadiz, Spain +34 (0)956 791 200 www.valderrama.com	Spain	
82	**Hamilton** St Andrews Terrace, Hamiltion, PO Box 10046, New Zealand +64 (07) 849 2069 www.hamilton.nzgolf.net	New Zealand	
83	**Royal Porthcawl** Royal Porthcawl Golf Club, Rest Bay, Porthcawl, Mid Glamorgan, CF36 3VW, Wales +44 (0)1656 782251 www.royalporthcawl.com *See page 146*	Wales	
84	**Spyglass Hill** Spyglass Hill Rd, Pebble Beach, California (CA) 93953, USA +1 831 625 8563 www.pebblebeach.com	USA	
85	**Scioto** Scioto Country Club, 2196 Riverside Drive, Columbus, Ohio (OH) 43221, USA +1 614 486 4341 www.sciotocc.com	USA	
86	**Gleneagles (King's)** Gleneagles Hotel, Auchterarder, Perthshire, PH3 1NF, Scotland +44 (0)1764 662231 www.gleneagles.com	Scotland	
87	**Somerset Hills** 180 Mine Mount Rd, Bernardsville, New Jersey (NJ) 07924, USA +1 908 766 0044	USA	
88	**Prestwick** Prestwick Golf Club, 2 Links Road, Prestwick, Ayrshire, KA9 1QG, Scotland +44 (0)1292 67102 www.prestwickgc.co.uk	Scotland	
89	**Machrihanish** Machrihanish Golf Club, Machrihanish, Campbeltown, Argyll, PA28 6PT, Scotland +44 (0)1586 810213 www.machgolf.com	Scotland	
90	**Durban (Country Club)** Durban Country Club, Durban, KwaZulu-Natal, South Africa +27 (0)31 313 1777 www.dcclub.co.za	South Africa	

TOP 100 GOLF COURSES CHECKLIST

Rank	Course	Location	Played
91	**Congressional (Blue)** 8500 River Rd, Bethesda, Maryland (MD) 20817, USA +1 (0)301 469 2032 www.ccclub.org	USA	☐
92	**East Lake** East Lake Golf Club, 2575 Alston Drive, Atlanta, Georgia (GA) 30317, USA +1 404 373 5722 www.eastlakegolfclub.com	USA	☐
93	**Naruo** 1—4 Kanegaya, Nishi-Uneno, Kawanishi-shi, Ikeda, Hyogo, Japan +81 727 94 1011	Japan	☐
94	**Maidstone** Old Beach Lane, East Hampton, New York (NY) 11937, USA +1 516 324 5530	USA	☐
95	**Harbour Town** Harbour Town Golf Links, The Sea Pines Resort, 32 Greenwood Dr, Hilton Head Island, South Carolina (SC) 29928, USA +1 800 925 4653 www.seapines.com	USA	☐
96	**Royal Melbourne (East)** Cheltenham Road, Black Rock, Victoria, 3193, Australia +61 3 9598 6755 www.royalmelbourne.com.au	Australia	☐
97	**Shoreacres** 1601 Shore Acres Rd, Lake Bluff, Illinois (IL) 60044, USA +1 847 234 1472	USA	☐
98	**Nanea** Nanea Golf Club, 75-1027 Henry St, Kailua Kona, Hawaii (HI) 96740, USA +1 (0)808 930 1300	HI/USA	☐
99	**Old Sandwich** Old Sandwich Golf Club, 44 Talcott Pines Rd, Plymouth, Massachusetts (MA) 2541, USA +1 (0)508 209 2270	USA	☐
100	**Ballyneal** Ballyneal, 216 South Interocean Avenue, Holyoke, Colorado (CO) 80734, USA +1 (0)970 854 5900 www.ballyneal.com	USA	☐

Nairn (6th hole), Scotland

PICTURE CREDITS

All images copyright Keith Baxter except for the following:

Cover: Shutterstock (www.shutterstock.com)
Endpapers, silhouettes and page 20: Shutterstock (www.shutterstock.com)
Page 2–3: Turnberry (Ailsa), Scotland / © Anthony Munter
Pages 6–7: Kingsbarns (12th hole), Scotland / © Andy Newmarch
Pages 32–33: Old Head (12th hole), Ireland / © Andy Newmarch
Page 44: Prince's, England / © Prince's Golf Club
Page 58: Gloria Resort, Turkey / © Andy Newmarch
Page 96: Moor Park clubhouse, England / © Andy Newmarch
Pages 120–1: Loch Lomond (9th hole), Scotland / © Loch Lomond Golf Club
Page 126: Kingsbarns (4th hole), Scotland / © Andy Newmarch
Page 131: St. Andrews (Old), Hell Bunker / © Jim McCann